NAVY ENVIRONMENTAL HEALTH CENTER
Technical Manual NEHC-TM PM 6250 1 (September 2000)

Navy Medical Department
Pocket Guide to
MALARIA PREVENTION
AND CONTROL

NAVY ENVIRONMENTAL HEALTH CENTER

BUREAU OF MEDICINE AND SURGERY

Navy Medical Department Pocket Guide to Malaria Prevention and Control

September 2000

Adapted from NEHC TM92-1 by

CDR James E. LaMar II, MC, USN; the Preventive Medicine Directorate, NEHC; and the Navy Preventive Medicine Community.

Navy Medical Department
Pocket Guide to
MALARIA PREVENTION AND CONTROL

TABLE OF CONTENTS

INTRODUCTION

The threat to health and readiness of sailors and Marines posed by malaria stimulated the creation of the Malaria "Blue Book" in 1984. Prevention and treatment of malaria is more complex due to the emergence of drug resistance, pesticide resistant mosquito vectors, and large populations of infected people in many areas of the world. The World Health Organization estimates that two billion people are at risk for malaria infection. Each year, malaria causes more than 300 million clinical cases and over two million deaths. In 1995, children under the age of five accounted for 800,000 of those deaths. The direct and indirect costs associated with malaria infections are enormous; costs were over 1.8 billion dollars in 1995 in Africa alone.

Malaria str kes during war, during deteriorating social and economic conditions, and after natural disasters; all situations where the military is called to serve. Deployed forces cannot afford loss of personnel or depletion of resources for cure and convalescence. Protecting and improving the health of airmen, soldiers, sailors, and Marines while serving in such operations requires thorough understanding of the prevention and treatment of malaria. This "Malaria Pocket Guide" includes information to help service personnel:

⇒ Understand the transmission and life cycle of malaria parasites.
⇒ Prevent malaria.
⇒ Diagnose and treat malaria.
⇒ Persuade commanders to enforce malaria preventive measures.

Command Responsibility

Malaria control depends on directed discipline by those in command. In their role as advisors, medical personnel must identify threats, and present countermeasures and their benefits so those in command can make effective decisions. In World War II, Lieutenant

General Sir William Slim stopped the longest, most humiliating retreat in the history of the British Army. When he assumed command in Burma in April 1942, the health of his troops was dismal. For each wounded man evacuated, 120 were evacuated with an illness. The malaria rate was 84 percent per year of total troop strength, even higher among the forward troops. In his memoirs, he describes his course of action:

> "... A simple calculation showed me that at this rate my army would have melted away. Indeed it was doing so before my eyes.
>
> Good doctors are of no use without good discipline. More than half the battle against disease is not fought by doctors, but by regimental officers. It is they who see that the daily dose of mepacrine (anti-malarial chemoprophylactic drug used in W.W.II) is taken...if mepacrine was not taken, I sacked the commander. I only had to sack three; by then the rest had got my meaning.
>
> Slowly, but with increasing rapidity, as all of us, commanders, doctors, regimental officers, staff officers, and NCOs united in the drive against sickness, results began to appear. On the chart that hung on my wall the curves of admissions to hospitals and malaria in forward units sank lower and lower, until in 1945 the sickness rate for the whole 14th Army was one per thousand per day."

The threat to force readiness that challenged General Slim and his army similarly confronts our forces today. In 1993, a large percentage of Marines and soldiers in certain units participating in Operation Restore Hope in Somalia developed malaria. The explanation for the outbreak is complex, involving a number of factors. The complex life cycle of malaria, lack of command support leading to poor execution of personal protective measures, and incomplete medical intelligence of the malaria threat all contributed.

Available medical intelligence concluded that *Plasmodium falciparum* was the predominant malaria threat in Somalia. Task Force medical planners were influenced by the Army's policy of not performing G-6-PD screening on its personnel. The risk of precipitating a hemolytic reaction from terminal primaquine prophylaxis had to be weighed against the chance that *P. vivax* and *P. ovale* were present. Based on those factors, Task Force medical planners did not recommend terminal primaquine prophylaxis.

Unfortunately, *P. vivax* was endemic in Somalia, and 75 soldiers developed malaria infections after they returned to the United States. After the first 30 soldiers were diagnosed with *P. vivax* malaria, terminal primaquine prophylaxis was instituted. Despite this precaution, another 45 soldiers developed malaria infections and had to be hospitalized and administered higher dosages of primaquine. Clearly *P. vivax* malaria is present in Somalia, and drug resistant strains are developing. It should be just as obvious that poor execution of personal protective measures allowed these soldiers to be bitten by infective mosquitoes. Returning Marines also developed *P. vivax* infections. The reasons were difficult to quantify, but poor compliance with terminal primaquine prophylaxis and resistant strains of *P. vivax* were responsible.

The story does not end with the *P. vivax* malaria outbreak in returning soldiers and Marines. During Operation Restore Hope, medical surveillance revealed that half of all malaria and dengue cases were occurring in a single Marine battalion located in the Baardera area. Investigation of these outbreaks found that the Marine commander did not enforce recommended countermeasures. Fortunately, consequences were minimal. The ill Marines recovered, and the unit was not involved in any significant engagements in its weakened condition.

The examples presented show that malaria is a formidable and deceptive foe to military units deployed into endemic areas. Resistant plasmodia strains exist in most areas of the world, and some species lie dormant and attack long after the threat is perceived to be absent. Drugs once commonly used to prevent and treat malaria are no longer effective. Persuading commanders to enforce personal protective measures is difficult. No vaccine is yet available, though a promising falciparum malaria vaccine is being tested.

However, all the necessary tools are present for successful prevention of malaria. Medical personnel must successfully communicate the threat. After convincing their commanders, medical personnel must teach, supervise, and practice personal protective measures. At the same time, they must be able to diagnose and treat personnel stricken with malaria. **It cannot be emphasized enough, as General Slim demonstrated, that success against malaria requires a unified effort enforced by commanders**.

CHAPTER ONE

MALARIA: Disease, Life Cycle, Distribution

Definition

Malaria is both an acute and chronic disease caused by protozoa of the genus *Plasmodium*. Four species cause human malaria: *P. falciparum*, *P. vivax*, *P. malariae*, and *P. ovale*. The protozoa are transmitted to humans by female mosquitoes of the genus *Anopheles*. (Transmission can also occur by direct inoculation of infected red blood cells via transfusion, needles, or congenitally). Some signs and symptoms of the illness are high fever, chills, headache, anemia, and splenomegaly. Most serious and fatal complications are caused by *P. falciparum*.

Life Cycle

The life cycle of malaria is complex (see Fig. 1-1) with developmental stages and corresponding symptoms differing according to the *Plasmodium* species involved (see Table 1-1). Sporozoites, the infective stage of plasmodia, are injected from the salivary glands of infected mosquitoes during feeding. Following inoculation, the sporozoites disappear from the blood within 30 minutes. Many are destroyed by white blood cells, but some enter liver cells.

Exoerythrocytic Phase. Sporozoites that enter liver cells multiply asexually in a process called exoerythrocytic schizogony. Thousands of uninucleate merozoites form, displacing the nucleus of the liver cell, but causing no inflammatory reaction in the liver. Eventually, invaded liver cells rupture, releasing thousands of merozoites into the bloodstream. This occurs 6 to 16 days after initial infection depending on the infecting *Plasmodium* species.

Dormant or Hypnozoite Phase. All infections due to *P. falciparum* and *P. malariae* have a single exoerythrocytic form. All infected liver cells parasitized with *P. falciparum* and *P. malariae* rupture and release merozoites at about the same time.

In contrast, *P. vivax* and *P. ovale* have two exoerythrocytic forms. The primary type develops, causes liver cell rupture, and releases merozoites just as described for *P. falciparum* and *P. malariae*. The other form, which develops concurrently, is known as the hypnozoite. Sporozoites that enter liver cells differentiate into hypnozoites that remain dormant for weeks, months, or years. At some future time, the hypnozoites activate and undergo exoerythrocytic schizogony, forming a wave of merozoites that invade the blood and cause a delayed case or a clinical relapse.

Erythrocytic Phase. Released merozoites invade red blood cells (erythrocytes), where they develop into trophozoites. After a period of growth, the trophozoites divide and develop, eventually forming 8-24 merozoites in each red blood cell. When this process is complete, the host red blood cells rupture, releasing mature merozoites. The symptoms associated with malaria occur at this point.

The merozoites then invade fresh erythrocytes and another generation of parasites develops in the same manner. This process occurs repeatedly during the course of infection and is called eryrthrocytic schizogony. The length of this development cycle differs according to the species of parasite, varying from 48 hours in vivax, ovale, and falciparum malaria, to 72 hours in *P. malariae* infections. In the early stages of infection there is no characteristic periodicity as groups of parasites develop at different times. The febrile episodes caused are inconsistent. Later, the erythrocytic schizogony development cycle becomes synchronized, and the febrile paroxysms become more consistent. Some merozoites differentiate into sexual forms (female macrogametocytes, male microgametocytes) and develop in invaded red blood cells.

Vector Phase. *Anopheles* mosquitoes feeding on infected hosts ingest sexual forms developing in red blood cells. The female macrogametocytes and male microgametocytes mature in the mosquito's stomach and combine forming a zygote that undergoes mitosis. The products of mitosis are ookinetes, which force themselves between the epithelial cells to the outer surface of the stomach, and form into small spheres called oocysts. The oocysts enlarge as the nucleus divides, eventually rupturing and releasing thousands of motile sporozoites into the body cavity. The sporozoites migrate to the salivary glands, making the female mosquito infective. The vector phase of the life cycle, called sporogony, is complete in 8 to 35 days depending on species and environmental conditions.

Environmental Factors. *Anopheles* mosquitoes are essential for development, multiplication, and spread of plasmodia. Therefore, any area harboring *Anopheles* mosquitoes may be at risk for

Table 1-1. Selected Characteristics of the Four Species of Human Malaria

	P. falciparum	P. vivax	P. ovale	P. malariae
Incubation days (range)	12 (9-14)	13 (12-17) or up to 6-12 months	17 (16-18) or longer	28 (18-40) or longer
Exoerythrocytic cycle (days)	5.5-7	6-8	9	12-16
No. of merozoites per liver cell	40,000	10,000	15,000	2,000
Erythrocytic cycle (hours)	48	42-48	49-50	72
Red blood cell preference	younger cells, but can invade cells of all ages	Reticulocytes	Reticulocytes	Older cells
Relapses	No	Yes	Yes	No
Fever periodicity (hours)	none	48	48	72
Febrile paroxysm length (hours)	16-36 or longer	8-12	8-12	8-10
Severity of primary attack	severe in non-immune	mild to severe	mild	mild

Drug Resistance	++	+	-	-

Figure 1-1. Malaria Life Cycle

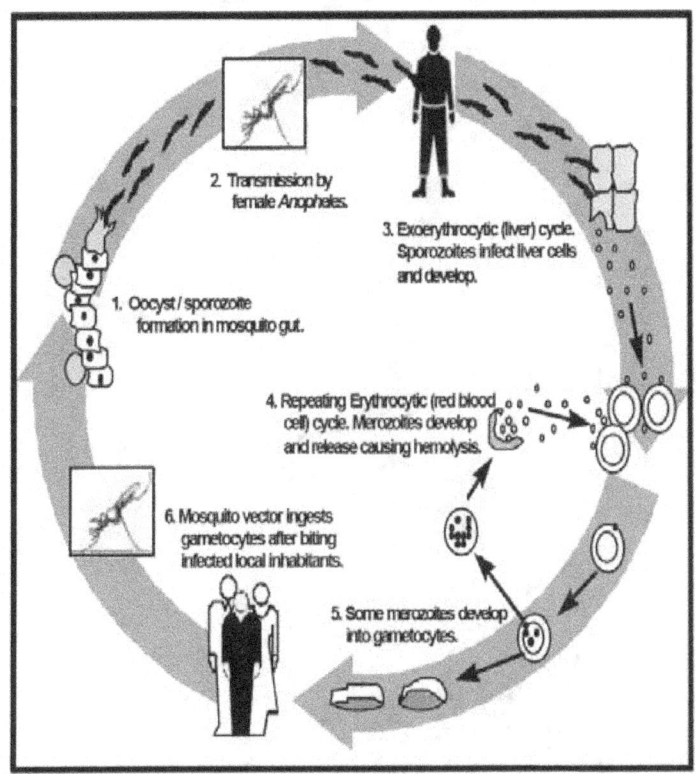

2. Transmission by female *Anopheles*.

3. Exoerythrocytic (liver) cycle. Sporozoites infect liver cells and develop.

1. Oocyst / sporozoite formation in mosquito gut.

4. Repeating Erythrocytic (red blood cell) cycle. Merozoites develop and release causing hemolysis.

6. Mosquito vector ingests gametocytes after biting infected local inhabitants.

5. Some merozoites develop into gametocytes.

malaria transmission. Specific environmental conditions optimal for anopheline mosquito vector and parasite development include temperature between 20^0 and 30^0C and a mean relative humidity of 60%. The sporogony phase requires temperatures between 16^0 and 33^0C. High relative humidity increases mosquito life-span, thereby increasing the probability of mosquitoes becoming infective. Areas with high rainfall have increased malaria incidence because of an increase in breeding sites. The accompanying high humidity increases survival rates of female anopheline mosquitoes. Elevation, along with cooler temperatures and lower humidity, is also a factor as transmission rarely occurs above 2000-2500 meters.

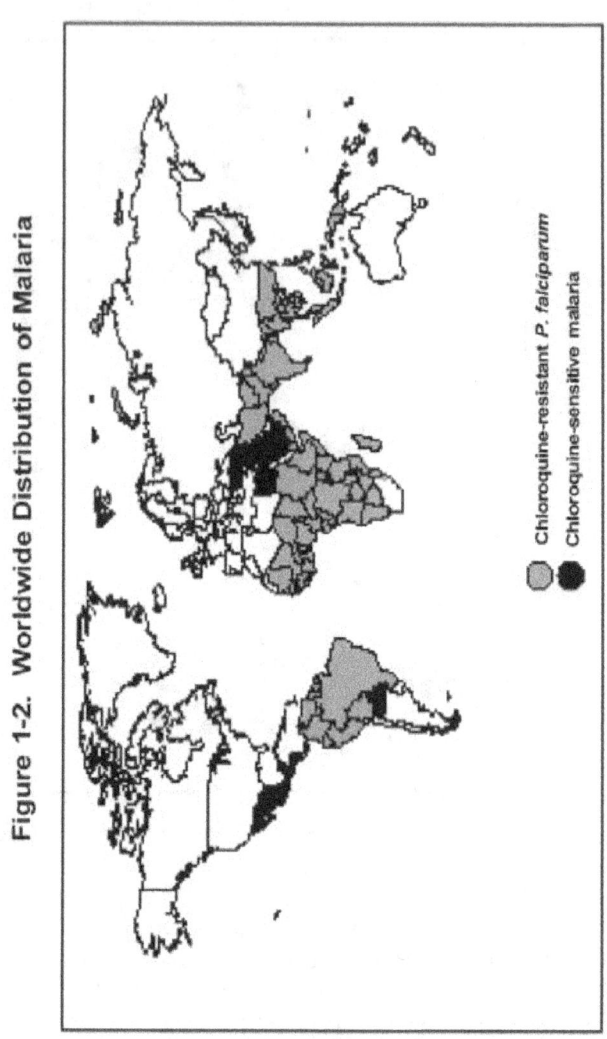

Figure 1-2. Worldwide Distribution of Malaria

○ Chloroquine-resistant *P. falciparum*
● Chloroquine-sensitive malaria

Distribution. The worldwide distribution of malaria is illustrated by the map in Fig 1-2. This is a general representation and not intended for threat assessment or countermeasure planning. Country-specific information can be obtained from the Medical Environmental Disease Intelligence and Countermeasures ("MEDIC") compact disc, and the

Navy Environmental and Preventive Medicine Unit respons ble for a particular world area. (Further intelligence can be obtained from the agencies listed in Appendix One).

Malaria transmission occurs in more than 100 countries. Regions include Africa, Asia, islands of the South, west, and central Pacific Ocean, Latin America, certain Caribbean islands, and Turkey. These areas, all between 45^0N and 40^0S latitude (see Fig. 1-2), possess tropical or subtropical zones wherein anopheline mosquito habitats exist.

CHAPTER TWO

PREVENTION

Systematic applications of four tactics are essential to planning and carrying out disease and injury prevention in field and combat operations. Listed in order, they are applicable for prevention of malaria (or any other threat):

1) Determine disease and injury threats in the area of operation before deployment.
2) Identify or develop countermeasures to reduce threats to an acceptable level.
3) Educate personnel regarding threats and train in correct use of countermeasures.
4) Command enforcement of countermeasures.

The next three sections of this chapter review effective malaria countermeasures available. Preventive countermeasures are divided into three sections: **Personal Protective Measures, Chemoprophylaxis,** and **Unit Protective Measures.** Medical personnel must seek information to answer the questions outlined below and determine which countermeasures to employ, and make recommendations for the same to commanders:

1) What type(s) of malaria is(are) present?
2) Which countermeasures will be effective in the area and situations the unit will encounter?
3) How will the unit obtain the necessary supplies, personnel, and equipment needed?
4) Do unit personnel know how to apply the countermeasures chosen? Will they apply them? What training is needed?
5) Does the entire chain of command understand its role and accountability in enforcing the countermeasures?

Section I. Personal Protective Measures

This section presents measures that prevent mosquitoes from biting and transmitting malaria. **Applications of personal protective measures are effective against a wide range of disease vectors, not solely for prevention of malaria.** In many military operations, they will be the **only** means of protection against biting arthropods. They are the first line of defense, are simple to teach and perform, and enable personnel to remain in endemic areas while maintaining their operational capabilities. The major drawback of personal protective measures is dependence on service member compliance. Persuasion by medical personnel, and enforcement by NCOs and commanders is necessary for their continuous proper application. Medical personnel must circulate among units teaching, examining, and improving personal protective measure practice, and also reporting their findings to those in charge. Commanders and NCOs must ensure compliance and lead via personal example.

DEET

Topical repellents are natural or synthetic compounds that repel arthropods. The use of vapor-active skin repellents by U.S. Armed Forces has a long history. It began with the use of oil of citronella in 1910, continued with the discovery of dimethyl phthalate during WW II, and led to the development of diethyl toluamide or "DEET" in 1957. The duration of a repellent's effectiveness decreases with activity, heat, and humidity. Since *Anopheles* mosquitoes inhabit warm tropical environments, military personnel need to re-apply repellent frequently to prevent biting. These products were selected based on their effectiveness. Contrary to public opinion, Avon Skin So Soft[R] and flea collars are not effective. **As with all repellents and insecticides, carefully read and comply with the label requirements.**

Available Military Supplies: Insect/Arthropod Repellent Lotion (NSN 6840-01-284-3982) is a 33 % DEET lotion developed to last 12 hours, has low odor, and less damaging to plastics than previous formulations. Apply in the same manner as skin lotion; neglected skin is not protected.

Insect Repellent, Clothing and Personal Application (NSN 6840-00-753-4963) is a 75% DEET, 25% alcohol liquid that must be applied every 1-2 hours in warm, humid conditions. It may cause skin irritation, is corrosive to plastics and paint, and is very flammable.

Apply in the same manner as skin lotion; neglected skin is not protected. The liquid can also be used as a fabric impregnant, with effectiveness of up to 2 days if not removed by laundering, rain, or perspiration.

Permethrin Uniform Impregnants

Impregnants are compounds very similar to topical repellents. They are longer lasting, and cannot be applied to skin. Permethrin is an impregnant for fabric only, used by the military to treat tents and clothing. It is also a contact insecticide capable of reducing the biting population and attack rate in the immediate area of use. Permethrin is a synthetic compound modeled from a naturally occurring insecticide found in certain plants. It is quick acting, long lasting (12 years in unwashed, stored clothing), nearly odorless, and non-staining. Permethrin is resistant to degradation when exposed to heat, sunlight, wear, laundering, rinsing, and immersion in water. It is effective against crawling arthropods such as ticks, and flying insects such as mosquitoes and biting flies.

Available Military Supplies: Permanone Aerosol Spray "Insect Repellent, Clothing Application" (NSN 6840-01-278-1336) is a formulation of 0.5% permethrin in 6 oz. aerosol cans for use on uniforms and mosquito netting. It is odorless, non-irritating, and can last through 3-5 washings. Apply the same way as spray paint (slow sweeping motion 6-8 inches from object) until the surface of the fabric appears moistened. Allow to dry for 2 hours before wearing. Do not apply to caps, socks or undergarments or while clothing is being worn.

IDAA Kit, "Insect Repellent, Clothing Application" (NSN 6840-01-345-0237) is a field kit in which shirt and trousers are treated in separate plastic bags containing a 1% permethrin and water mixture. Treatment lasts through about 30 washings.

Protective Clothing and Netting

The basic utility or camouflage uniform treated with permethrin and worn with sleeves down, collars closed and trousers bloused over boots offers excellent protection from mosquitoes. Other types of protective clothing and netting are also available.

Available : DEET net jacket, known as Parka, Fabric Mesh, Insect Repellent, (NSN 8415-01-035-0848) is a waist length mesh jacket with extra long sleeves and a hood designed to cover a combat helmet. The fabric is polyester netting interwoven with cotton strands designed to absorb DEET. It is issued with a ziplock plastic bag and a bottle of the 75% DEET liquid (NSN 6840-00-753-4963). Before wearing, saturate the coat with the supplied DEET and store in the plastic bag for 24 hours. Protection should last 6 weeks if the jacket is stored in the ziplock pouch when not being worn. Impregnation with permethrin is also an option, which provides longer, more effective protection.

Insect Head Net (NSN 8415-00-935-3130) is a fine mesh nylon screen and cover that can be worn over a helmet, cap, or bare head. It is designed to be fastened to the uniform shirt collar and breast pocket buttons. For maximum protection, impregnate with permethrin or DEET liquid.

Mosquito Bed Nets, (NSN 7210-00-266-9736), and poles (NSN 7210-00-267-5641) are a protective measure with a long history of use in tropical areas. They are designed for use with cots, bedrolls, hammocks, steel beds, and shelter half tents. Personnel should receive bed nets and be trained in their use before entry into an endemic area. If set up properly, they will not interfere with quick night exits. Bed nets should be treated with permethrin, set up before dusk and checked for tears or other spots where mosquitoes can enter. A training team to coach, inspect, and advise on the application of personal protective measures including bed net use should be established for each unit.

Section II. Chemoprophylaxis

This section presents three frequently used chemoprophylactic regimens. Choice of regimen is determined by two factors:

⇒ Drug resistance in specific locations.
⇒ Any allergic or other reaction to the anti-malarial drug of choice, or restriction by job (mefloquine is not authorized for prophylaxis in aviators and divers).

Excellent primary sources of information on malaria drug resistance are the Medical Environmental Disease Intelligence and Counter-Measures ("MEDIC") compact disc, and the Navy Environmental and Preventive Medicine Unit responsible for that area of the world. (Agencies dedicated to supplying such information, along with all needed contact information and protocol are listed in Appendix 1).

Unit personnel must be screened before malaria chemoprophylaxis is initiated. Personnel who had prior reactions or risk factors, and those in certain occupations need to be identified and provided with an appropriate regimen.

Chemoprophylaxis: Before, During, After. One of the least appreciated aspects of chemoprophylaxis is the requirement for taking the drug before, during, and after exposure to malaria. Chemoprophylaxis should begin 2 weeks before travel to endemic areas to allow adequate blood levels to develop. This is true for all malaria prophylaxis drugs except for doxycycline, which should be initiated 1-2 days before exposure. The two-week lead-time is also useful to monitor personnel for any drug reactions. Prophylaxis must be continued for four weeks after leaving an endemic area to ensure that suppressive cure results. The required four week time period is to ensure drug therapy exceeds the length of time needed for the incubation period in the liver. If a mosquito bites on the last day of deployment, protection is needed 2-3 weeks later, when parasites emerge into the blood stream.

Directly Observed Therapy (DOT). Directly observed therapy is recommended for all regimens. Chain of command support is required to carry out this method. A fellow service member supervised by a chain of command authority observes weekly or daily drug dosage.

Chemoprophylactic Regimens. The three regimens are descr bed below; doses are listed in Table 2-1:

Regimen A. For areas where chloroquine resistant *P. falciparum* has NOT been reported, once weekly use of <u>chloroquine</u> alone is recommended. Chloroquine is usually well tolerated, and the few personnel who have side effects may tolerate the drug better by taking it with meals, or in divided twice-weekly doses.. Chloroquine 500 mg salt (300 mg base)/wk should begin 2 weeks before entering endemic areas of operation, taken once a week while deployed, and once a week for four weeks after leaving. The related drug, hydroxychloroquine, is useful as an alternative and may be better tolerated. It is available by open purchase under the trade name Plaquenil[R].

Regimen B. For areas where chloroquine resistant *P. falciparum* exists, <u>mefloquine</u> is recommended. Mefloquine is usually well tolerated at prophylactic dosage, but should not be taken by personnel with a history of seizures, severe psychiatric disorders, or those with cardiac conduction abnormalities. Aviators are proh bited from using it. Mefloquine 250 mg/wk should begin 2 weeks before entering endemic areas of operation, taken once a week while deployed, and once a week for four weeks after leaving.

   If a two-week lead time prior to exposure is not possible, a loading dose of 250 mg/day on days 1, 2, 3, and 7 may be given. This is followed by the routine weekly regimen. This short interval loading dose period has been used with very few side effects. If this regimen is chosen, medical personnel should monitor unit members for side effects.

Regimen C. <u>Doxycycline</u> is also recommended for areas where chloroquine- resistant *P. falciparum* exists. If given under supervision, it is very effective. Doxycycline

Table 2-1. Drugs Used for Malaria Prophylaxis*

Drug	Adult Dosage	Pediatric Dosage
Mefloquine (Lariam[R])	250 mg salt (228 mg base), once/week	15-19 kg: 1/4 tab/wk 20-30 kg: 1/2 tab/wk 31-45 kg: 3/4 tab/wk > 45 kg: 1 tab/wk
Doxycycline	100 mg once/day	> 8 yr. of age: 2 mg/kg once daily, up to adult dose of 100 mg/day
Chloroquine phosphate (Aralen[R])	500 mg salt (300 mg base), once/week	5 mg/kg base (8.3 mg/kg salt), once/wk up to maximum adult dose of 300 mg base
Primaquine	15 mg base (26.3 mg salt), once/day for 14 days	0.3 mg/kg base (0.5 mg /kg salt), once/day for 14 days (maximum 15 mg base)
Hydroxychloroquine sulfate (Plaquenil[R])	400 mg salt (310 mg base), once/week	5 mg/kg base (6.5 mg/kg salt), once/week up to maximum adult dose of 310 mg base
Proguanil (Paludrine[R])	200 mg, once/day, in combination with weekly chloroquine	< 2 yr.: 50 mg/day 2-6 yr.: 100 mg/day 7-10 yr.: 150 mg/day >10 yr.: 200 mg/day

*all are oral doses

100 mg/day is taken at approximately the same time of day, beginning 1-2 days before entering endemic areas of operation, taken daily while there, and daily for four weeks after leaving. It is the drug of choice for chemoprophylaxis in most parts of Southeast Asia.

One of the most common side effects of doxycycline is adverse gastrointestinal symptoms, usually nausea or vomiting. This often leads to compliance problems. These side effects may be avoided by taking doxycycline with a meal. Other side effects include photosensitivity manifested by a severe sunburn reaction, and an increased frequency of monilial vaginitis. The sunburn reaction can be prevented by avoiding prolonged exposure to sunshine, or sunscreen use. Females taking doxycycline should be supplied with nystatin suppositories to treat possible yeast infections when they occur.

Terminal Primaquine Prophylaxis: Currently, primaquine is the only available drug for prevention of *P. vivax* and *P. ovale* relapse. As most endemic areas of the world have at least one of these species, terminal primaquine prophylaxis is recommended to eradicate hypnozoites. It can be initiated immediately or soon after personnel depart the area of exposure, or during the last two weeks using Regimens A, B, or C. This ensures an overlap of medication to eradicate parasites of any stage that may be present. No other medication eliminates *Plasmodia* merozoites in the liver. Without primaquine therapy, personnel can harbor dormant parasites in the liver long after leaving the risk area. Terminal primaquine prophylaxis is given to ensure a complete cure.

Dosage is 15 mg base (26.3 mg salt)/day for 14 days; DOT recommended. Dosage may need to be increased to 30 mg if resistant *P. vivax* and *P. ovale* strains are present in the area. Personnel should be screened for G-6-PD deficiency before given primaquine. See Chapter 6 for details and recommendations. In certain instances, terminal primaquine prophylaxis may not be indicated. Consult with the cognizant Navy Environmental and Preventive Medicine Unit or other authorities for recommendations on need for terminal primaquine prophylaxis or increased dosages.

Prophylaxis During Pregnancy: Women who are pregnant should avoid travel to malarious areas. When travel must occur, chloroquine is safe to use in pregnancy. No harmful fetal effects have been reported when given in the recommended doses for malaria prophylaxis. Proguanil has been used for several decades without adverse effects on the pregnancy or fetus.

Mefloquine is not recommended for use during pregnancy by the FDA. However, a review of clinical trials and reports of inadvertent use during pregnancy shows no association with adverse fetal or pregnancy outcomes. Mefloquine may be considered for use by females who are pregnant when exposure to chloroquine-resistant *P. falciparum* is unavoidable.

Doxycycline is contraindicated for malaria prophylaxis during pregnancy. Fetal effects include discoloration and dysplasia of teeth and inhibition of bone growth. Tetracyclines are only indicated to treat life-threatening infections due to multi-drug resistant *P. falciparum*.

Primaquine should not be used during pregnancy, as it can be passed transplacentally to a G-6-PD deficient fetus, causing in utero hemolytic anemia. Chloroquine can be given once weekly until delivery, at which time primaquine can be given.

Pediatric Prophylaxis: Children should avoid travel to areas with chloroquine-resistant *P. falciparum*, unless a highly effective drug such as doxycycline or mefloquine can be administered. Indications and dosage schedules are the same as for adults; dose is based on age or weight (see Table 2-1).

Doxycycline is contraindicated in children under 8 years of age. Mefloquine is not recommended in children who weigh less than 15 kg, though recent data suggest it is safe for use in that group. Chloroquine and proguanil are safe for pediatric use.

Chloroquine is manufactured in the U.S. in tablet form only, and has a very bitter taste. Pharmacists can pulverize tablets into powder for mixing in food or drink, or prepare gelatin capsules. Oral suspensions of chloroquine are available overseas; parents should calculate dose because preparations vary. Overdose of anti-malarial drugs can be fatal. They must be stored in childproof containers out of reach of children.

Section III. Unit Protective Measures

Unit malaria protective measures consist of the following:

⇒   Discipline and training.

⇒ Treatment of equipment with permethrin.
⇒ Camp selection.
⇒ Vector control measures.

Discipline and Training

Avoiding malaria, other diseases, and non battle injuries is a team effort that must be supported by command authority. Medical personnel must be prepared to decisively advise those in command of such threats and their countermeasures, train personnel in the use of protective measure use, and monitor their application and effectiveness. Disciplined and correct use of the personal protective measures thus far presented is very effective in preventing malaria and other diseases.

Equipment Treatment

Units should institute a program to treat uniforms, netting, and tents with Insect Repellent, Clothing Application (NSN 6840-01-334-2666). This is a 40% concentrate in 5.1 oz. bottles that is mixed with water and applied using a 2-gallon sprayer to uniforms, netting, or tents. Other gear (camouflage netting, ground covers, sleeping bags, hammocks, and window drapes) should also be treated.

Treat tents while erected, and uniforms and miscellaneous items while spread on the ground. Treated uniforms are ready to wear when dry; do not treat underwear or caps. Mark date of treatment on items. Permethrin is very long lasting (12 years in unwashed, stored clothing), and such treatment could be done during routine field exercises. This approach would effectively prepare unit equipment months or years before use in an actual contingency.

Effectiveness in uniforms lasts through 30 washings. Tents and netting should be retreated every 6-9 months if regularly used. The impregnation of miscellaneous items (camouflage netting, ground covers, sleeping bags, hammocks, window drapes, and barrier nets) for protection is very effective.

Camp Selection

If the tactical situation permits, base camps should be located in areas where there is low risk of exposure to infected mosquitoes. The following factors affect the risk of exposure:

⇒ Presence of mosquito breeding sites.
⇒ Direction of prevailing winds.
⇒ Proximity of settlements with malaria infected inhabitants.
⇒ Length of time unit will be present in area.

Breeding areas vary depending on the specific species of *Anopheles* mosquito responsible for malaria transmission. Sunlit streams, shaded lagoons, rice fields, and marshes are all breeding habitats for different species of *Anopheles* mosquitoes. Campsite selection close to possible breeding sites of the mosquito known to transmit malaria in that region should be avoided. When camping near an area where a high density of *Anopheles* mosquitoes is unavoidable, camp where the prevailing winds will blow the mosquitoes away from camp.

A host population of infected humans is necessary to infect mosquitoes. If possible, locate base camps distant enough from settlements with infected inhabitants so as to be beyond normal flight range (2-3 kilometers) of the *Anopheles* mosquito vector .

Duration of deployment in the area is also important for planning permanent mosquito control measures. If military presence may be prolonged, establishment of a long-term base should be done with the preceding factors in mind or where elimination of mosquito breeding areas through engineering and control projects is feasible. Entomologists should be consulted to find the site most amenable for development by determining mosquito activity and identifying breeding areas. Improvement projects that impound water should be screened by entomologists and preventive medicine personnel to prevent creation of mosquito breeding areas.

Another unit protective measure to consider when operating in endemic areas is reducing troop exposure during peak biting times (dusk till dawn for most anophelines). Examples include:

1) Restrict showers and baths to hours when the mosquitoes are not biting.
2) Reschedule work parties and unit formations.
3) Allocate available screening material to buildings that protect the largest number of personnel during peak mosquito biting times.

Malaria Vector Control Measures

Vector control includes two stages: surveillance and control. First, mosquito surveillance and analysis of collected data are performed. The analysis leads to choice of control measures most applicable to area and situation. Mosquito control is the employment of chosen vector control measures.

Preventive medicine teams deployed in contingency situations are prepared to survey campsites for mosquitoes and other vectors, determine their breeding areas, and establish programs to control them. They are experienced at implementing sanitation and other public health measures and prepared to supervise and provide technical guidance to unit personnel (medical and non-medical) on unit protective measure management, if needed. These teams include medical entomologists.

Medical entomologists supervise the two-stage process, first determining mosquito species, their abundance, and breeding sites. A control plan is then recommended, including specific control methods and their evaluation. Descriptions of common vector surveillance and control techniques used by medical entomologists follow.

Mosquito Surveillance Techniques

Larval Mosquito Surveys. The goals of sampling for mosquito larvae are to identify their habitats, and later to evaluate control measures. All possible breeding areas are checked by sampling a uniform volume of water, and counting and identifying larvae present. From these data, the larval index, or average number of larvae collected per sample is calculated and recorded. This information is used to justify the use of permanent control measures such as filling or draining.

Anopheles larvae are found in areas of heavy surface vegetation where debris accumulates, usually in water less than one meter deep. In larger ponds or lakes, they are found close to the shore.

Adult Mosquito Surveys. These are most frequently done because adult mosquitoes are often easier to collect and identify. These surveys determine the species present and their relative abundance, and the potential of a disease outbreak. For example, if no species of *Anopheles* mosquitoes are collected, the risk of malaria transmission will probably be low.

Biting Collections and Landing Counts. This is the most simple and direct method used to determine which vector species in a region is feeding on humans. Relative abundance, host preference, place and time of biting, and species are estimated. Mosquitoes are vacuumed into a container when they land. Counts continue for a designated period of time (usually 15-30 minutes). A standard area of skin is exposed, and the data are converted to "bites per man per hour" of each species collected for standard comparison.

Success of mosquito control measures can be evaluated by comparing biting counts before and after application of mosquito control measures. The same "bait" collector, and location should be used for each collection to assure comparability of results.

A landing count survey is done to rapidly assess mosquito biting activity and abundance when populations are high. An index (landing rate) is obtained by recording the number of mosquitoes that land on clothing within a certain time interval (usually one minute).

Resting Sites. Daytime inspections are useful for some anopheline mosquitoes. They rest in cool, dark, humid places protected from the wind during the day. From these sites, they are vacuumed into a container and provide a representative sample of the population.

Pyrethrum Spray/Sheet Collection. Spread white sheets on the floor of a human or animal shelter and spray the overhead spaces above with pyrethrum or 2% d-phenothrin. Any mosquitoes resting overhead will be killed, and can be collected from the sheets and identified. For best results, the technique should be used during midmorning hours.

Light Traps. Light traps are the most widely used method to sample adult mosquito populations. The New Jersey light trap has limited use in military situations because of its size and need for a 110 volt power source. The solid state Army miniature light trap is more often used in the military setting. Traps are hung near wooded areas, swamps, or potential breeding sites, 5-6 feet above ground and 30 feet away from buildings, avoiding areas exposed to strong winds or artificial light sources. They are scheduled a specific number of nights per week, and results are tabulated as to species, sex, and total number collected per night, per location. A trapping index (total females divided by number of trap nights) will detect changes in the population density of mosquitoes in an area.

Some *Anopheles* mosquito species are not attracted by light, but by carbon dioxide (CO_2). If so, light traps are baited with a perforated container of dry ice mounted above the trap. Light traps and adult mosquito resting counts are initially unsatisfactory to monitor populations of *Anopheles* mosquitoes because these methods may not identify all potential vector species. Mosquito collections from landing counts should be done until medical entomologists are satisfied that they have identified all *Anopheles* species present in the area. Then, they determine which collection methods are sufficient to monitor area species.

Mosquito Control Measures. The goal of malaria vector control is to eliminate the anopheline population or reduce it below the number required to sustain disease transmission. There are three main methods used to reduce mosquito populations:

⇒   Biological control.
⇒   Elimination of breeding sites.
⇒   Insecticides.

The use of insecticides to kill larvae and adult mosquitoes has been practiced in many military operations. Elimination of breeding sites and employment of biological control methods may take too long to have an effect or are too resource intensive to be practical in most military operations. However, they are quite effective as public health measures for control of malaria and may be employed in humanitarian operations.

Biological control. Several methods of biological control currently exist. One involves the introduction of *Bacillus thuringiensis israelensis*, a mosquito bacterial pathogen, into a targeted mosquito population. Another requires the introduction of mosquito larvae-eating fish, *Gambusia* spp., into breeding areas.

Elimination of breeding sites. Breeding sites can be made unsuitable for mosquito larvae through a variety of methods. They include increasing water flow or ditching, removing protective aquatic vegetation, or other actions that completely destroy breeding areas (filling or draining). Aside from limiting water containers in bivouac areas or simple ditching to provide drainage, permanent removal of breeding sites requires careful and thorough engineering, heavy equipment, and personnel usually not available to an engaged military force.

Insecticides: Chemical Control of Larvae. Treatment of standing water with larvicides provides temporary control of mosquitoes and is more effective than adult control techniques. Unfortunately, the adult mosquito population is not immediately affected. Therefore, this may be a cost effective control method if troops are going to be located in the area for an extended period.

Solutions, emulsifiable concentrates, and suspensions are effective with ground operated or aerial dispersal equipment. They are also available in forms that can be applied by hand (briquettes or biodegradable plastic pouches). Medical entomologist supervision is essential. Considerations include larvicide formulation, delivery method, and amount and application rate. Method, amount, and formulation vary depending on geography, vegetation, species, level of insecticide resistance, and possible toxic effects on local inhabitants and troops in the treatment area.

Insecticides: Chemical Control of Adult Mosquitoes, Outdoor Control. The treatment of choice to control adult mosquitoes is ultra-low-volume spraying (ULV). ULV spraying provides adequate protection for limited periods of time. To provide continuous protection in large areas with many breeding sites, ULV insecticides must be applied on a repetitive schedule, typically twice daily, daily, or every other day.

ULV insecticides should be applied when winds are calm (less than 6 knots), and when the ground is cooler than the air. Such temperature conditions usually occur at sunrise and sunset. However, many Anopheles mosquitoes are most active later in the evening. As ULV insecticides are most effective against flying insects, spraying operations should be planned for dusk, after dark, and early morning (near sunrise). When properly applied, ULV treatments do not leave dangerous or unsightly deposits on trees, bushes, or terrain.

Aerial application of insecticide requires special consideration. It requires the authorization of certified Department of Defense entomologists or applied biologists, and qualified pest control personnel must supervise the operation. Factors considered before use include size of treatment area, vegetation cover (canopy) and density, suitability of alternate measures, prevalence of vector borne diseases, and the prospects of increasing troop effectiveness.

Insecticides: Chemical Control of Adult Mosquitoes, Indoor Control. Indoor control of mosquitoes relies on aerosol space sprays that have only a short-term effect. They must be re-applied whenever new mosquitoes enter the space.

Another method of indoor control is application of residual sprays to surfaces where mosquitoes rest. Use permethrin or a long lasting spray recommended by a medical entomologist. For porous surfaces such as brick or unfinished wood, use a suspension made with a water-mixable powder or a microencapsulated formulation.

Insecticides: <u>Chemical Control of Adult Mosquitoes</u>, <u>Barrier Treatments</u>. Residual spray treatment of all vegetation surfaces within 30 meters of small camps or bivouac areas can establish a barrier against mosquito re-infestation. Apply with backpack or hand held sprayers.

CHAPTER THREE

DIAGNOSIS

The definitive diagnosis of malaria is made by the identification of malaria parasites in a peripheral blood film. However, U.S. medical professionals are inexperienced in malaria diagnosis and treatment because they rarely encounter the disease. When confronted with malaria, Navy medical personnel have misdiagnosed it as "viral illness", "gastroenteritis", or "flu." Malaria also may not be considered because it shares signs and symptoms with other tropical illnesses including typhoid fever, rheumatic fever, and bacterial meningitis. Therefore, diagnosis of malaria requires a raised level of suspicion and diligent screening.

Screening. Screen all febrile patients possibly exposed to malaria transmission. This includes personnel who took malaria chemoprophylaxis medication while deployed to endemic areas, or air crew or travelers briefly exposed at airports in malaria endemic zones.

The screening tool of choice for malaria diagnosis is microscopic examination of thick and thin blood smears. Thick smear examination detects the presence of any organisms; thin smear examination identifies the specific infecting *Plasmodium* species. Thick and thin smears can be prepared on the same microscope slide; see Appendix 3 for description of this technique and further information on preparing and interpreting peripheral blood smears.

Timing of Screening. Symptoms often precede detectable parasitemia by 1-2 days. Therefore, screen blood obtained through fingersticks or other techniques several times a day (frequency is more important than timing) until a diagnosis of malaria is made or ruled out. Thin smear diagnosis for causal species is crucial, as *P. falciparum* infections are life threatening and require specific treatment. After diagnosis, blood smears should continue to be monitored for response to therapy. Decreasing parasite count (concentration) signifies favorable response to therapy; frequency of testing depends on therapeutic response and severity of illness. For example, seriously ill patients should be tested 2-3 times daily until they significantly improve, then daily until parasite level is zero.

Early diagnosis and treatment is lifesaving; falciparum malaria kills 25% of non-immune adults within 2 weeks if treatment is not started early in the infection. **If the diagnosis of malaria is suspected, treat, then arrange for definitive diagnosis.** The rest of this chapter describes the clinical manifestations of malaria to aid in early diagnosis and understanding of disease processes.

Clinical Manifestations

Symptoms (Table 3.1). Patients present with a variety of symptoms depending on the stage of infection and the infecting species. Fever is virtually always present, and fever plus any other symptom might be malaria if exposure occurred. Common complaints include mild to moderate malaise, fatigue, muscle aches, back pain, headache, dizziness, loss of appetite, nausea, vomiting, abdominal pain, and diarrhea. Dry cough and shortness of breath have been reported in some patients. Gastrointestinal complaints can be considerable, suggesting a diagnosis of gastroenteritis. Young children and semi-immune individuals may complain of fever and headache as their only symptoms.

Signs. Physical examination usually demonstrates an increased temperature, tachycardia, and warm flushed skin. The spleen is often palpable in initial infection, but this is more likely in subsequent attacks. It is usually soft and may be tender. The liver is often enlarged and may be tender; jaundice is not unusual. Orthostatic hypotension often occurs during initial infections. Mental confusion and cyanosis are sometimes encountered.

Laboratory Findings (Table 3.2). Abnormal laboratory findings reflect the severity of hemolysis. Blood. A normocytic, normochromic anemia with leukopenia and thrombocytopenia is sometimes present on initial screening, but is almost always present following medication therapy with the resultant clearing of parasitemia. Massive *P. falciparum* infections cause acute decreases in hemoglobin, hematocrit, and an increase in reticulocyte count. Kidneys. Trace to moderate protein, urobilinogen, and conjugated bilirubin may be found on urinalysis. In severe *P. falciparum* infections, massive hemolysis

Table 3-1. Malaria Clinical Findings

Sign or Symptom	Percent with Finding
• Fever & Chills	96
• Headache	79
• Muscle Pain	60
• Palpable Liver	33
• Palpable Spleen	28
• Nausea & Vomiting	23
• Abdominal Cramps/Diarrhea	6

combined with circulating immune complexes produces acute renal insufficiency or failure ("blackwater fever") with laboratory findings of hemoglobinuria, proteinuria, and an elevated serum creatinine. Fever and dehydration may cause an increase in BUN and creatinine, but if serum creatinine rises disproportionately higher than BUN (BUN to creatinine ratio is normally 10 or 12 to 1), renal failure must be considered.

Liver. Liver impairment may occur, though hyperbilirubinemia normally results from hemolysis. Abnormalities in liver function tests, increased ALT, AST, and prolonged prothrombin time, sometimes occur causing diagnostic confusion with viral hepatitis. Serum albumin is usually decreased.

Hypoglycemia, commonly seen in *P. falciparum* infections and pregnancy, is due to the 75-fold increase in glucose consumption by parasitized red blood cells. In addition, quinidine or quinine may stimulate insulin secretion, causing clinically significant hypoglycemia when used for treatment, especially when given intravenously. If a patient deteriorates during convalescence, especially with a deterioration in neurologic function, hypoglycemia should be considered as a possible cause.

False positive serologic tests may be present, including syphilis (VDRL, RPR), rheumatoid factor, heterophil agglutinins, and cold agglutinins. These result from

Table 3-2. Malaria Laboratory Findings

Finding	Normal Range	Percent with Abnormal Findings

• Reticulocytosis	3 - 18%	42
• Thrombocytopenia	12K-150K	36
• Bilirubin Increased	1 - 1.8	33
• VDRL Positive	(-)	28 (+)
• Anemia	5.8 - 12 (Hgb)	28
• Leukopenia	3,000 - 4,700	26
• Alk. Phos. Increased	11-27	17
• SGOT Increased	40 - 108	10

a polyclonal increase in both IgG and IgM immunoglobulins, which are associated with appearance of specific malarial antibodies and reduced complement levels. Malaria does not cause eosinophilia.

Hyperparasitemia. Patients with *P. falciparum* infections that are hyperparasitemic have a higher risk of death. Hyperparasitemia is defined as a parasite count of greater than 250,000 per microliter (>250,000/?l), or as having greater than 5% of red blood cells parasitized. Risk of death is due to extensive microvascular disease, and severe metabolic effects from the parasite load.

Pathophysiology and Clinical Presentation

Clinical symptoms and signs of malaria occur shortly before or at the time of red blood cells lysis. Fever is caused by the release of merozoites, malarial pigment, parasite proteins and cellular debris. Chills or rigor, followed by high fever occur in a cyclical pattern in infections due to *P. vivax*, *P. ovale*, and *P. malariae*, but not *P. falciparum*, which is more likely to show continuous fever with intermittent temperature spikes. Clinical signs and symptoms described are those experienced by non-immune patients, such as will be seen in most U.S. military personnel. Clinical manifestations are not as severe in persons living in endemic areas. They are infected intermittently and develop partial immunity.

The malaria paroxysm is the defining clinical feature of the disease. That being said, it is often not present. Fever caused by malaria can have any pattern, and falciparum infections often present with a constant fever. The classic paroxysm typically has three stages, and is preceded in some patients by an initial period of nonspecific symptoms. Those symptoms include fatigue, muscle aches, loss of appetite, headache, and a slight fever of 2-3 day's duration.

A paroxysm begins with the "cold" or "chilling" stage lasting 15 minutes to several hours during which the patient feels cold and has shaking chills. The second "hot" stage lasts several hours and coincides with red blood cell rupture and merozoite release. During the second stage temperatures rise to $40^{\circ}C$ ($104^{\circ}F$) or higher. There is minimal sweating and the patient is at risk of febrile seizures or hyperthermic brain damage. Clinical signs and symptoms include tachycardia, hypotension, cough, headache, backache, nausea, abdominal pain, vomiting, diarrhea, and altered consciousness. Within 2-6 hours, the patient enters the third "sweating" stage of the paroxysm with generalized sweating, resolution of fever, and marked exhaustion, usually giving way to sleep. Paroxysms occur in regular intervals, but take several days to emerge.

As previously stated, the classic paroxysm described above is generally not how *P. falciparum* infections present. *P. falciparum* malaria is more severe and qualitatively different from the other plasmodia that infect humans, and is the only type that causes microvascular disease. For those reasons, it will be discussed separately and in more detail.

Malaria due to *Plasmodium falciparum* Infection

Plasmodium falciparum malaria is a microvascular disease with a substantial metabolic element that damages tissue in the following manner: *P. falciparum* parasites mature in red blood cells causing knobs to form on their surface in effect making them "sticky". This stickiness causes parasitized red blood cells to adhere to endothelial cells, lining capillaries and postcapillary venules of brain, kidneys, and other organs, obstructing blood flow. In addition to being "sticky," infected red blood cells are less flexible, adding to their obstructive potential. In obstructed capillaries and postcapillary venules, parasites consume glucose and produce lactate-causing acidemia and release of tissue necrosis factor-? (a cytokine produced by the immune system). Lack of oxygen and increased concentrations of toxic metabolites cause capillaries to become more permeable, allowing leakage of protein and fluids. This results in tissue edema and further anoxia due to the edema, leading to organ damage and death. In some cases, diagnosis of *P. falciparum* infection is made difficult because no parasites are seen on peripheral blood smears, as they are sequestered in the host's microvasculature.

Cerebral Malaria. The principal manifestations of cerebral malaria are seizures and impaired consciousness, usually preceded by a severe headache. Neurologic examination may be unremarkable, or have findings that include contracted or unequal pupils, a Babinski sign, and absent or exaggerated deep tendon reflexes. Cerebrospinal fluid examination shows increased pressure, increased protein, and minimal or no pleocytosis. High fever, 41^0 to 42^0C (106^0 to 108^0F), with hot, dry skin as seen in heat stroke can occur.

Manifestations of cerebral malaria are caused by microvascular obstruction that prevents the exchange of glucose and oxygen at the capillary level, hypoglycemia, lactic acidosis, and high-grade fever. These effects impair brain function, yet cause little tissue damage in most cases, as rapid and full recovery follows prompt treatment. Ten to twelve percent of patients surviving cerebral malaria have persistent neurologic abnormalities upon hospital discharge.

Renal Failure. Renal failure, due to acute tubular necrosis, is a common complication of severe *P. falciparum* infections in non-immune persons. Acute tubular necrosis in severe *P. falciparum* infections is caused by two mechanisms: renal tubules become clogged with hemoglobin and malarial pigment released during massive hemolysis, and microvascular obstruction causes anoxia and glucose deprivation at the renal capillary or tissue level. Failure of urine production is a poor prognostic sign, requiring peritoneal or hemodialysis.

Pulmonary Edema. Often fatal, acute pulmonary edema can develop rapidly and is associated with excessive intravenous fluid therapy. Fast, labored respiration, with shortness of breath, a non-productive cough, and physical findings of moist rales and rhonchi are usually present. Chest X-rays usually show increased bronchovascular markings. It is thought that the pulmonary edema is more related to release of tissue necrosis factor, than to the effects of microvascular obstruction.

Gastroenteritis. Most patients with falciparum malaria complain of loss of appetite and nausea. However, in some patients (especially young children), additional symptoms including vomiting, abdominal pain, watery diarrhea, and jaundice are present leading to misdiagnosis of viral gastroenteritis or hepatitis. Clinical manifestations are associated with the adherence of parasitized red blood cells in the microvasculature of the gastrointestinal tract.

Anemia. Destruction of red blood cells upon merozoite release, and inhibition of hematopoesis by tissue necrosis factor-? cause the severe anemia often seen in *P. falciparum* infections. Also, *P. falciparum* parasites can infect red blood cells of all ages, which theoretically allows infection of all circulating red blood cells. Whereas, *P. vivax* and *P. ovale* require young red blood cells (reticulocytes) and *P. malariae* requires mature blood cells for infection.

Severe anemia is defined as a hematocrit of less than 21%, and clinical manifestations may include dark brown or red urine (hemoglobinuria), decrease in urine production, and jaundice. Renal failure, as previously discussed, may be a complication. Another cause of hemolysis and hemoglobinuria in patients with malaria is destruction of G-6-PD deficient red blood cells by oxidant anti-malarial drugs such as primaquine.

Malaria due to *P. vivax* (or *P. ovale*) Infection

Infections due to *P. vivax* and *P. ovale* are virtually the same. Both are less severe than falciparum malaria, and parasite blood levels are lower. Parasitized red blood cells do not develop knobs, therefore no microvascular obstruction with resultant brain, kidney, lung, or other organ complications occur in malaria due to *P. vivax* or *P. ovale*.

P. vivax and *P. ovale* form a dormant stage in liver cells called hypnozoites. These parasites activate and cause delayed infections or a relapse (Table 3-3). A relapse usually occurs within 6 months of an acute attack. Some hypnozoites remain dormant much longer, and are virtually undetectable. If there is any suspicion that *P. vivax* or *P. ovale* is endemic in the area of exposure, presumptive treatment must be given to prevent illness. Currently, the only available treatment is primaquine; dosages are listed in Chapters 4, 5, and Appendix 4.

As previously stated, fever is virtually always present, and fever plus any other symptom might be malaria. *P. vivax* or *P. ovale* fevers may be erratic or continuous in the initial phase of illness. After 3 to 4 days, if not treated, the fever then develops into a synchronous cycle of afternoon temperature increases every 48 hours. The fever can be as high as $40^{\circ}C$ ($104^{\circ}F$), and symptoms during this stage have been described as worse than falciparum malaria. Physical findings usually include an enlarged, tender spleen, and a palpable liver present by the second week of infection. Deaths have been reported due to rupture of an enlarged spleen.

Parasitemia levels are less for *P. vivax* or *P. ovale* because they infect only young red blood cells, unlike *P. falciparum* which can infect red blood cells of all ages. Fewer red blood cells are hemolyzed, but their loss stimulates replacement. This increases the number of young red blood cells (reticulocytes), which are susceptible to infection, leading to parasitemia levels greater than 1 to 2% in *P. vivax* or *P. ovale* infections.

Malaria due to *P. malariae* Infection

P. malariae infection is the mildest and most chronic of all the human malaria infections. Invasion of red blood cells builds up slowly, so blood parasite levels are low, and symptoms are usually mild. Patients may have several febrile paroxysms before parasites are seen in the peripheral blood. As in *P. vivax* and *P. ovale* infections, febrile paroxysms develop in the afternoon, but cycle every 72 hours. *P. malariae* and *P. falciparum* do not have the hypnozoite stage, therefore relapses do not occur in infections with these species. Recrudescence can be seen with *P. malariae* infections many years after the initial infection. This is due to an increase in parasites after a chronic, low level of parasitemia in infected red blood cells that have persisted in tissue microcapillary circulation. Low-grade infections can persist up to 20-30 years. Splenomegaly is a common complication in those patients with low-grade infections of long duration.

P. malariae infection may produce a unique immune complex glomerulonephritis . Low-level parasitemia causes continuous antigen stimulation of host antibodies and formation of immune complexes, causing an immune complex glomerulonephritis. This manifestation usually presents 3-6 months after malaria transmission season, and can lead to nephrotic syndrome. Half the people who develop nephrotic syndrome had their first symptoms before the age of 15. Classic findings include persistent proteinuria, hypoalbuminemia, edema, and ascites. Patients who develop this complication do not respond to anti-malarial therapy, and response to corticosteroids is variable.

Table 3-3. Characteristics of malaria relapse and recrudescence.

	Relapse or Delayed Illness	Recrudescence

Species	P. vivax, P. ovale	P. malariae
Cause	hypnozoites (persistent liver cell stage)	persistent undetectable parasitemia

Malaria in Pregnancy

Because of the immune suppression associated with pregnancy, recrudescence and relapse are frequent in the second and third trimester. Malaria can potentiate the anemia of pregnancy, and cause acute renal insufficiency and hypoglycemia in P. falciparum infections. It is associated with increased numbers of abortions, miscarriages, stillbirths, and neonatal deaths.

Malaria in Children

In non-immune children, the initial attack can vary widely. Common symptoms include drowsiness, anorexia, thirst, headache, nausea, vomiting, and diarrhea. Common early signs include increased temperature (may be greater than $40^{\circ}C$), pallor, and cyanosis; enlarged liver and spleen occur later. Convulsions are frequent, and cerebral malaria is the most frequent complication. Anemia is a complication with repeated infections.

Children living in endemic areas develop limited immunity. Symptoms are milder and more difficult to detect. They include low-grade anemia, restlessness, loss of appetite, weariness, sweating, and intermittent fever.

CHAPTER FOUR
TREATMENT

Overview

After establishing the presence of a malaria infection, treatment should be initiated as soon as possible. Specific treatment regimen depends on whether the case is diagnosed as complicated or uncomplicated malaria. Severity of clinical illness and level of parasitemia determine this distinction. In addition, steps must be taken to identify the responsible species, and the area where transmission occurred as those factors influence treatment. Patients diagnosed with complicated malaria are at risk for morbidity and death. Prompt treatment minimizes this risk. If possible, treatment of malaria should be done in consultation with a physician trained and experienced in treatment, with access to a tertiary care center.

Choice of treatment regimen, drug type, and selection of oral or intravenous administration, is based on the above factors. Two types of drugs are used to treat malaria. *Blood schizonticides*, which attack parasites in red blood cells, are used in acute infection to prevent or terminate the clinical attack. *Tissue schizonticides* are medications that act on the exoerythrocytic parasite stages (forming merozoites and hypnozoites) in liver cells to prevent relapse. Treatment with *tissue schizonticides*, known as "radical" cure, is required for infections of *P. vivax* and *P. ovale*. An algorithm for malaria treatment is illustrated in Figure 4-1.

During treatment, patients must be monitored for response to therapy and complications from the infection or treatment. Repeated clinical assessment is important in cases of severe malaria, where early detection of complications and immediate intervention may be lifesaving.

Figure 4-1. Algorithm for Treatment of Malaria

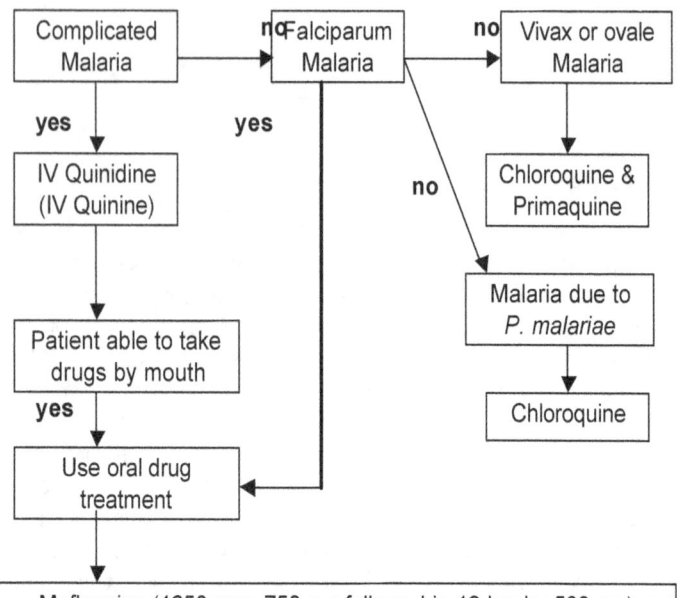

1. Mefloquine (1250 mg: 750 mg followed in 12 hrs by 500 mg), or
2. Halofantrine (500 mg q 6 hrs x 3 doses, repeat in 7 days), or
3. Quinine (600 or 650 mg tid to complete 7 days of therapy for complicated; or 600-650 mg for 3-7 days for uncomplicated), *plus either*
   - Doxycycline 100 mg bid; or Tetracycline 250 mg qid to complete 7 days of therapy; or
   - Pyrimethamine/sulfadoxine (Fansidar[R]) (3 tablets in a single dose on last day of quinine.)

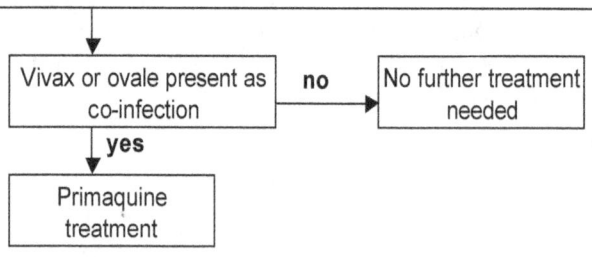

Table 4-1. Uncomplicated Malaria Treatment

DRUG	DOSE	
Chloroquine-sensitive		
Chloroquine	Adults: 1.0 gm (600 mg base) initially, 500 mg (300 mg base) in 6 hrs, then 500 mg (300 mg base) at 24 and 48 hrs Children: 10 mg base/kg, 5 mg base/kg 6 hrs, later, then 5 mg base/kg at 24 and 48 hrs	
Chloroquine-resistant		
Mefloquine* *or*	Adults: 1250 mg (750 mg followed in 12 hrs by 500 mg). Children: 25 mg/kg once (15 mg/kg followed in 8-12 hrs by 10 mg/kg).	
Halofantrine *or*	Adults: 500 mg every 6 hrs x 3 doses, not with meals*. Repeat dose in 7 days. Children (<40kg): 8 mg/kg every 6 hrs x 3 doses. Repeat dose in 7 days	
Quinine *plus either*	Adults: 600 or 650 mg of the salt tid for 3-7 days. Children: 25 mg/kg/day of the salt divided into 3 doses x 7 days.	
Doxycycline* *or* Fansidar^R (500 mg sulfadoxine, 25 mg pyrimethamine)	Doxy :100mg bid x 7 days; do not use in children under 8. For children over 8, doxy 2 mg/kg bid x 7 days; not to exceed 100mg bid. Adults: 3 tablets in a single dose. Children: ¼ tab < 1 yr, ½ tab 1-3 yrs, 1 tab 4-8 yrs, 2 tabs 9-14 yrs, 3 tabs > 14 yrs, all single dose.	

* contraindicated for use in pregnant or lactating women, and those at risk of cardiac arrhythmia

Treatment

Uncomplicated Malaria. Chloroquine remains the medication of choice for patients with *P. vivax, P. ovale, P. malariae*, and uncomplicated chloroquine-sensitive *P. falciparum* infections. Drugs and dosages for treatment of uncomplicated malaria are listed in Table 4-1. Chloroquine-resistant *P. vivax* has been reported in New Guinea, Indonesia, Myanmar, India, Irian Jaya, and the Solomon Islands; so it is important to consult with medical intelligence sources to obtain the latest information on drug resistance in the area of transmission. Chloroquine is safe, and the 3-day treatment course is well tolerated. If chloroquine therapy is not effective, or if infection was acquired in an area with chloroquine-resistant malaria, mefloquine is the next drug of choice, followed by quinine in combination with either doxycycline or pyrimethamine-sulfadoxine (Fansidar^R). Tetracycline may be used as an alternate to doxycycline. The regimen of tetracycline is an adult dose of 250 mg qid, and a pediatric dose of 5 mg/kg qid, not to exceed 250 mg qid. Doxycycline and tetracycline are not to be used in children under 8. For uncomplicated malaria, quinine can be given as a 3 day course, except in Southeast Asia where a 7 day course is required because of an increase in relative resistance to quinine.

Febrile, acutely ill patients are prone to vomiting anti-malarial drugs, which are very bitter tasting. Administer an antipyretic such as Tylenol^R (acetominophen). This eases symptoms and helps patients tolerate anti-malarial drugs. Patients continuing to vomit require treatment by injection, administration of crushed tablets via nasogastric tube, or suppository. After administering an effective dose by one of these routes, patients can usually complete their course of therapy by mouth.

Complicated Malaria. Complicated malaria is almost always due to *P. falciparum*, and is associated with a mortality rate between 15 and 25%. Its diagnosis is based on the severity of clinical manifestations and a parasitemia involving more than 1% or 2% of red blood cells. Patients presenting with any of the clinical manifestations listed in Table 4-2 should be treated for complicated malaria. Drugs and dosages for treatment of complicated malaria are listed in Table 4-3.

Treatment approach for complicated malaria is listed below:
- Start treatment as soon as diagnosis is suspected.
- Calculate dosage according to patient weight.

- Give medication intravenously.
- Give loading dose of medication (not indicated if patient has received quinine, quinidine, or mefloquine in the last 24 hours).
- If patient is comatose, place on his or her side and give a single parenteral dose of Phenobarbital (5-20mg/kg) to prevent convulsions.
- Measure parasite count and hematocrit every 6-12 hours.
- Exchange transfusion is indicated for patients with high level parasitemia (>15%) and should be considered for severely ill patients with parasitemia levels between 5 to 15% if it can be provided safely.
- Switch to oral medication as soon as patient can tolerate tablets, and response to treatment is confirmed.
- Observe patients carefully for drug toxicity and complications.

Patients with complicated malaria should be treated with intravenous quinidine (parenteral quinine has not been available in the U.S. since 1991). Intravenous quinine or quinidine are potent blood schizonticides, and therapeutic plasma concentrations can be quickly and safely achieved by administration of a loading dose. Loading doses have been shown to decrease the duration of fever, parasitemia, and coma, and should be given if the patient has not received quinine, quinidine, or mefloquine in the last 24 hours.

Loading doses of quinine or quinidine should be given followed by continuous infusion. Baseline blood pressure and ECG should be obtained before initiating therapy, and periodically throughout treatment. Therapy should be discontinued if systolic blood pressure persists below 80 mm Hg, if either the QRS interval widens greater than 50% of baseline or the QT interval is greater than 0.6 seconds; or if a cardiac arrhythmia arises.

Overdose of quinine or quinidine, particularly if too rapidly infused, can cause convulsions, hypotension, cardiovascular collapse, heart block, and ventricular fibrillation. If possible, plasma concentrations of quinidine or quinine should be monitored, and the maintenance dose should be reduced if plasma concentrations exceed 20µg/ml(mg/l). The maintenance dose should be reduced to one-third to one-half after 48 hours to prevent accumulation and toxicity, unless the patient has improved and can tolerate oral medication. Therapeutic doses of both quinine and quinidine can cause hypoglycemia through stimulation of insulin release. All patients treated with intravenous quinidine or quinine should receive a continuous infusion of 5 to 10 % dextrose.

Measure blood glucose periodically during treatment, every 4 to 6 hours in unconscious patients, and give prompt treatment of intravenous dextrose if glucose levels fall below 40mg/dl (2.2mmol/l).

Table 4-2. Manifestations of Complicated Malaria

MAJOR SIGNS	DESCRIPTION
Unarousable coma	Failure to localize or abnormal response to painful stimuli; coma persisting for >30 min after generalized convulsion
Seizures	More than two generalized convulsions in 24 hours
Severe anemia (normochromic, normocytic)	Hematocrit rapidly falling or <15%, or hemoglobin <5g/dl, with parasitemia level > 10,000 per ml, or with > 1 to 2% of RBCs involved
Severe bleeding abnormalities	Significant bleeding from gums, nose, GI tract, and/or evidence of disseminated intravascular coagulation
Pulmonary edema /adult respiratory distress syndrome	Shortness of breath, fast labored respiration, rales
Renal failure	Urine output <400 ml/24 hrs (<12 ml/kg per 24 hrs in children); no improvement with re-hydration; serum creatinine >3.0 mg/dl (>265 ?mol/l)
Hemoglobinuria	Black, brown, or red urine; not associated with effects of drugs or red blood cell enzyme defects (primaquine/G-6-PD)
Hypoglycemia	Glucose <40mg/dl (<2.2 mmol/l)
Hypotension/shock	Systolic BP <50 in children aged 1-5 or <80 in adults; core to skin temperature >10^{0}C difference
Acid base disturbances	Arterial pH <7.25 or plasma bicarbonate <15 mmol/l

Table 4-3. Regimens for treatment of Complicated Malaria

Drug	Dose (Pediatric dose same unless indicated)
IV Therapies	
Quinidine gluconate	10 mg of base/kg loading dose (max. 600 mg) in normal saline infused over 1-2 hours, followed by 0.02 mg/kg/min continuous infusion until oral therapy can be started.
Quinine dihydrochloride (available only outside the U.S.)	20 mg/kg loading dose IV in 5% dextrose over 4 hrs, followed by 10 mg/kg over 2-4 hrs q8h (max. 1800 mg/d) until oral therapy can be started.
Oral Therapies	
Mefloquine* Or	Adults: 1250 mg (750 mg followed in 12 hrs by 500 mg); Children: 25 mg/kg (15 mg/kg followed in 8-12 hrs by 10 mg/kg).
Halofantrine Or	Adults: 500 mg q 6 hrs x 3 doses, repeat in 7 days; Children: 8 mg/kg q 6 hrs x 3 doses, repeat in 7 days.
Quinine Plus either Doxycycline Or Fansidar[R] (500 mg sulfadoxine, 25 mg pyrimethamine)	Adults: 600 or 650 mg salt tid; Children: 25 mg/kg/d in 3 doses x 3-7d. Adults: Doxy 100 mg bid, not indicated for children under 8. Children over 8: doxy 2 mg/kg bid, not to exceed 100 mg bid. Adults: 3 tablets in a single dose. Children: ¼ tab < 1 yr, ½ tab 1-3 yrs, 1 tab 4-8 yrs, 2 tabs 9-14 yrs, 3 tabs > 14 yrs, all single dose.

*delay initial dose until 12 hours after the last dose of quinidine or quinine

Intravenous therapy is continued until the patient is able to tolerate oral therapy. Regimens for oral therapy are given in Table 4-3. Tetracycline may be used as an alternate to doxycycline. The regimen of tetracycline is an adult dose of 250 mg qid, and a pediatric dose of 5 mg/kg qid, not to exceed 250 mg qid. Doxycycline and tetracycline are not to be used in children under 8.

Alternate treatments include intravenous chloroquine, intramuscular Fansidar^R, mefloquine or halofantrine tablets crushed and mixed with water given via nasogastric tube, or artemisinin derivatives. Intravenous chloroquine is less toxic than quinine or quinidine, but resistance to it is so prevalent that it is not used for treatment of severe malaria cases. This applies even to areas without resistant strains of malaria. If oral therapy with mefloquine is chosen to complete the recommended 7 days of therapy, delay the intial dose for 12 hours after the last dose of quinidine or quinine.

Halofantrine is a newly licensed drug developed by the Walter Reed Army Institute of Research. It should not be used in patients who developed *P. falciparum* infections while on mefloquine prophylaxis because parasite resistance to both drugs is similar. In addition, fatalities have occurred when halofantrine has been used for treatment in patients who received mefloquine prophylaxis.

Intramuscular Fansidar^R (a combination drug containing sulfadoxine and pyrimethamine) has been shown to clear parasitemia as quickly as chloroquine, but hypersensitivity reactions to sulfonamides are common and cause complications.

Artemisinin, a compound known as qinghaosu in China, has been used with great success there and in trials in Thailand. It is available as heterogeneous compounds in suppository, intravenous, and tablet forms.

"Radical" Cure. To prevent relapse, *P. vivax* and *P. ovale* infections need to be treated to eradicate tissue schizonts (persistent liver cell stages known as hypnozoites). This is known as "radical" cure, and currently the only available effective drug is primaquine. It is a potent oxidant, and can cause severe hemolytic anemia in G-6-PD deficient patients. Therefore, before treating with primaquine, the G-6-PD status of patients must be checked, and an appropriate dosage regimen selected. Radical cure dosage schedules are listed in Table 4-4.

Table 4-4. Primaquine Treatment Regimens

G-6-PD NORMAL	1 tablet* per day x 14 days
G-6-PD deficiency (Mild African form)	3 tablets per week for 8 weeks
G-6-PD deficiency (More severe Mediterranean variety)	2 tablets per week for 30 weeks

* 1 tablet consists of 26.3 mg pimaquine phosphate, 15 mg primaquine base.

Treatment Management

Monitoring. Complicated malaria patients are at risk for sudden decompensation and need to be closely monitored. If possible, these patients should be transferred to facilities with an intensive care unit (ICU) or equivalent. Treatment should be supervised by a physician. Initial patient monitoring should be frequent (every 1 to 2 hours), until the patient improves. Parameters to monitor include:

- Vital signs (temperature, pulse, blood pressure, respiration)
- Parasite concentration.
- Urinary output.
- Serum electrolytes.
- Blood glucose.
- Hematocrit/hemoglobin.
- ECG (required for quinidine treatment).

Response to therapy is monitored by serial blood smears. Fewer parasites will be seen on successive smears if treatment is effective. If no improvement in clinical symptoms or decrease in parasitemia is seen in the first 24 to 48 hours of treatment, resistance should be assumed and treatment with an alternate drug should be initiated. Providers should be vigilant and monitor other parameters to identify the common complications of malaria: cerebral malaria, hypoglycemia, anemia, renal failure, pulmonary edema, concurrent bacterial infection, and over-hydration. Prompt initiation of supportive measures (intravenous hydration, glucose administration, oxygen therapy, blood transfusion, etc.) is important in reducing permanent injury and mortality.

Cerebral Malaria. Generalized seizures occur in more than 50% of patients with cerebral malaria, and can lead to sustained neurological deterioration or aspiration pneumonia. Patients with impaired consciousness should be placed in the lateral decubitis position. If patient is unconscious, intubation with an endotracheal tube or placement of a rigid oral airway is indicated to maintain the airway. Vital signs, level of consciousness (modified Glasgow coma scale, see Table 4-5), and seizures should be monitored and recorded frequently. Seizures must be treated promptly with a benzodiazepine drug (diazepam, chlormethiazole, or lorazepam). A nasogastric tube should be placed to lower risk of aspiration pneumonia.

Deepening coma or signs of cerebral herniation are indications for further assessment with computed tomography (CT) or magnetic resonance imaging (MRI). If such techniques are not available, therapy to lower intracranial pressure should be attempted. Acceptable treatment measures include intravenous mannitol, 1.5 mg/kg of 10-20% concentration given over 30 minutes, or hyperventilation to reduce arterial pCO_2 below 4.0 pKa. Steroids have been proven ineffective when used in an attempt to lower intracranial pressure.

Seizures may be prevented with a single intramuscular dosage of phenobarbital sodium (loading dose 15-20 mg/kg, total dose 60-200 mg/kg/day). In an ICU, an alternate method is phenytoin, 10-15 mg/kg loading dose, followed by an adult maintenance dose of 100 mg every 6 hours. Plasma phenytoin concentration should be monitored daily.

Hypoglycemia. This complication should be suspected in any patient who becomes unresponsive. Frequent monitoring of blood glucose is necessary in complicated malaria, particularly during intravenous quinine or quinidine administration. Hypoglycemia can be caused by two mechanisms, stimulation of insulin release caused by quinine or quinidine therapy, or from consumption of glucose by large numbers of parasites. If available, give a therapeutic trial of 50% dextrose followed by continuous infusion of 5 or 10 % dextrose solution.

Table 4-5. Modified Glasgow Coma Scale

		Score
Best Verbal Response:	Oriented	5
	Confused	4
	Inappropriate words	3
	Incomprehensible sounds	2
	None	1
Best Motor Response:	Obeys commands	6
	Localizes pain	5
	Flexion to pain:	
	Withdrawal	4
	Abnormal	3
	Extension to pain	2
	None	1
	Total	**2 - 11**
	Unarousable coma	**≤ 7**

Pulmonary Edema. This complication results from either increased capillary permeability or fluid overload and resembles Adult Respiratory Distress Syndrome (ARDS). A patient with pulmonary edema needs treatment in an ICU, as positive pressure ventilation with positive end expiratory pressure/continuous positive airway pressure (PEEP/CPAP) is needed for adequate oxygenation. Fluid overload must be prevented by maintaining the central venous pressure between zero and 10-15 cm H_2O. If an ICU setting is not available, oxygen should be delivered by the most effective means available, and a rapid acting diuretic such as furosemide should be given intravenously.

Renal Failure. Renal complications are seen in one third of adult patients with severe falciparum malaria. Most patients will respond to cautious re-hydration with an increase in urine output. Dialysis is indicated for hyperkalemia, uremia, metabolic acidosis, or pulmonary edema. Treatment of intravascular hemolysis (blackwater fever) involves correction of uremia with dialysis, and avoidance of fluid overload due to blood transfusion. In cases of renal failure due to massive hemolysis, blood transfusion is usually necessary to prevent death.

Anemia. In most cases no intervention beyond treatment of the malaria infection is required. Transfusion should be considered if the hematocrit drops below 20%, or if it is falling rapidly and associated with clinical distress. Clinical manifestations indicating need for transfusion include shock, cardiac failure, hypoxia, and extreme lethargy.

Transfusion has safely been used to correct anemia, but the volume given must be included in fluid balance calculations to prevent pulmonary edema. Diuretics (furosemide, 1-2 mg/kg) can be given to promote urine output to maintain fluid balance during transfusion. Plasma expanders (colloids), and administration of oxygen can be used if transfusion is not practical or available.

Exchange transfusion for treatment of hyperparasitemia has been used for approximately 70 patients. Though most showed clinical improvement during and after the procedure, it has not been proven superior to optimal anti-malarial medication treatment. Manual exchange transfusion (alternating phlebotomy with transfusion), or continuous cell separation (hemophoresis) are methods of exchange transfusion that have been used.

Septic Shock. Secondary bacterial infection is a frequent complication in severe malarial cases. Blood, urine, and CSF fluid, etc. should be routinely cultured. Broad-spectrum intravenous antibiotics combining an aminoglycoside and a later generation cephalosporin should be started immediately if a secondary bacterial infection is suspected. Other causes of shock to consider are hypovolemia from dehydration, pulmonary edema, or massive blood loss (gastrointestinal hemorrhage or ruptured spleen).

Ruptured Spleen. This potentially fatal complication should be considered in patients infected with *P. vivax* or *P. falciparum*. Clinical manifestations include complaints of abdominal pain, especially in the left upper quadrant, left shoulder pain, and hypotension without other signs of blood loss. Free blood in the peritoneal cavity or a torn splenic capsule can be detected by ultrasound or CT, and confirmed by needle aspiration of the peritoneal cavity. A trial of conservative management is currently recommended so the spleen and its immunological functions can be preserved. This includes blood transfusion, close observation in an ICU or equivalent setting, and rapid access to surgical consultation.

Pregnancy. Treatment is essential for pregnant women to save their lives and prevent miscarriages. Falciparum malaria is associated with low birth weight, fetal distress, premature labor, miscarriage, stillbirth, and hypoglycemia. Treat as for any adult, suspect hypoglycemia, and do not give tetracycline or halofantrine.

Pediatrics. Most of the 1 to 3 million deaths from malaria each year are children, primarily in Africa. Common complications are convulsions, coma, hypoglycemia, metabolic acidosis, and severe anemia. Severe jaundice, acute renal failure, and pulmonary edema are unusual. Children tolerate anti-malaria drugs well, and treatment is virtually the same as for adults with appropriate dosage adjustments. Tetracycline drugs cause defects in forming teeth and bone, and should not be given to children under 8 or 9 years.

Completion of Treatment

Complicated malaria should be treated for a total of 7 days. Mefloquine can be given as a single dose when oral drugs can be tolerated, since therapeutic blood levels last for a week. Dosages of other oral medications indicated after intravenous therapy are shown in Table 4-3.

Uncomplicated malaria requires 3 days of chloroquine treatment in suscept ble infections. Oral mefloquine or halofantrine can be used in resistant cases. If *P. vivax* or *P. ovale* were identified or suspected, "radical" cure to eradicate hypnozoites is indicated. Table 4-4 lists appropriate dosages for patient G-6-PD status.

Follow Up and Prognosis

Once elimination of parasites has been documented on peripheral blood smears, routine repeat smears are not recommended. Patients should be advised that malaria relapse is possible despite thorough treatment. If presenting for care with a febrile illness within a year, they should be advised to inform their provider that they were recently treated for malaria and it should be considered a potential cause of their present illness.

CHAPTER FIVE

GLUCOSE-6-PHOSPHATE DEHYDROGENASE DEFICIENCY

Overview

The recognition of Glucose-6-Phosphate Dehydrogenase (G-6-PD) deficiency was the direct result of investigations of the hemolytic effect of the drug primaquine in the 1950s. G-6-PD is the first enzyme of the hexose monophosphate shunt, a biochemical pathway crucial in the protection of red blood cells. Damage done to hemoglobin molecules (See Table 5-1) by oxidizing drugs or chemicals is neutralized or reversed by substances that the hexose monophosphate shunt produces.

Primaquine is the only currently available drug able to destroy dormant hypnozoites in liver cells and prevent relapse of *P. vivax* or *P. ovale* malaria. Unfortunately, it is a strong oxidizing agent, and can cause severe hemolytic anemia in G-6-PD deficient personnel. In the U.S. military population, 2 types of G-6-PD deficiency are common. Understanding the difference between these types, and the primaquine treatment schedules available for each, can minimize or prevent complications from drug reactions, and allow treatment of the relapsing forms of malaria.

Physiology of G-6-PD Deficiency

Red blood cells are normally protected from oxidizing substances in a complex chemical pathway in which G-6-PD is an essential enzyme. In G-6-PD deficient red blood cells, this protective mechanism is compromised and oxidizing substances produced by infections or oxidant drugs damage hemoglobin molecules. In this harmful process, hemoglobin is denatured irreversibly and precipitates in clumps of protein called *Heinz bodies*. Heinz bodies attach to red blood cell membranes, deforming the cells, and are filtered from circulation by the spleen. Free hemoglobin is released into the blood

Table 5-1. Summary of Hemolysis in G-6-PD Deficiency

• Exposure of hemoglobin to oxidant
• Heinz body formation (denatured clumps of hemoglobin inside red blood cells)
• Deformation of red blood cells caused by attachments of red cell membranes and Heinz bodies
• Removal and destruction of deformed red bloods cells by the spleen
• Decline in hemoglobin, hematocrit
• Increase in red blood cell production (reticulocytosis) to compensate for decrease in red blood cells
• Hemoglobinuria and symptoms if hemolysis severe (overcomes the liver's ability to metabolize hemoglobin breakdown products)

from the destroyed red blood cells. If a large number of red blood cells are destroyed, the human body's normal compensatory mechanisms are overwhelmed. The amount of hemoglobin released into the bloodstream may be too great to be absorbed and metabolized by the liver, resulting in hemoglobinuria and kidney damage. Anemia may also occur if the loss of red blood cells is too great to be compensated by an increase in the rate of reticulocytosis. The extent of hemolysis depends on the type and severity of G-6-PD deficiency, and the amount of exposure to oxidizing substances (see Table 5-2).

G-6-PD Types. The gene for G-6-PD is located on the X chromosome(s). Severe deficiency is fully expressed in males and rare in females. Over 200 variants have been identified. In the U.S. military, the two types that are often encountered are G-6-PD $^{A-}$, found in 16% of Afro-American males, and the more rare G-6-PD^{Med} found in Greeks, Sardinians, Sephardic Jews, Arabs, and other males of Mediterranean descent.

Table 5-2. Drugs and Chemicals that Should be Avoided by G-6-PD Deficient Individuals

Acetanilid	Primaquine
Furazolidone	Sulfacetamide
Methylene blue	Sulfamethoxazole (Gantanol^R)
Nalidixic acid	Sulfanilamide
Naphthalene	Sulfapyridine
Niridazole (Ambilhar^R)	Thiazolesulfone
Isobutyl nitrite	Toluidine blue
Nitrofurantoin (Furadantin^R)	Trinitrotoluene (TNT)
Phenazopyridium (Pyridium^R)	Urate oxidase
Phenylhydrazine	

As normal red blood cells age, the activity of G-6-PD decays slowly, reaching 50% of its original level in 60 days. Despite this loss, normal red blood cells retain enough activity to sufficiently protect red blood cells from oxidants. G-6-PD decay is significantly pronounced in deficient individuals. G-6-PD^A declines to 50% of baseline activity in 13 days, while G-6-PD^{Med} declines to 50% of baseline activity in 1-2 days. In G-6-PD^A deficiency, young red blood cells have normal enzyme activity, while older cells are grossly deficient. In G-6-PD^{Med} virtually all red blood cells are deficient. Thus, hemolysis is self limited in individuals with G-6-PD^A, ending when older red blood cells are destroyed. In G-6-PD^{Med} hemolysis is much more severe, as all red blood cells are at risk (see Table 5-3).

Most cases of drug induced hemolytic reactions related to G-6-PD^A deficiency are probably sub-clinical. During the Vietnam War, only 20 persons were documented to have developed a severe drug reaction because of G-6-PD deficiency. At that time, chloroquine-primaquine tablets were given weekly to service members as malaria prophylactic therapy, and routine G-6-PD testing was not done. As thousands of service members were required to take the weekly prophylaxis, 20 cases were much less than expected. It is probable that the reactions that occurred were due to G-6-PD^{Med}, not G-6-PD^A.

Table 5-3. Clinical Comparison: G-6-PD ^{A} and G-6-PD^{Med}

	G-6-PD ^{A}	G-6-PD^{MED}
Frequency	Common in Afro-American populations	Common in Mediterranean populations
Degree of Hemolysis	Moderate	Severe
Hemolysis with: 　Drugs 　Infection	 Unusual Common	 Common Common
Need for transfusions	No	Sometimes
Chronic Hemolysis	No	No

Signs and Symptoms of Hemolysis. Signs and symptoms appear 1-3 days after initiation of drug therapy. Shortness of breath, rapid pulse, hemoglobinuria (brown or black urine), and fatigue are common clinical manifestations. In mild cases, shortness of breath, rapid pulse, and fatigue appear during or after physical exertion. A modest decline in hemoglobin (3-4 mg/dl) occurs without hemoglobinuria. Most of these cases are easily overlooked unless caregivers are alert.

If hemolysis is markedly severe, shortness of breath, rapid pulse, palpitations, and fatigue can present at rest. Some patients complain of abdominal or back pain. Signs include hemoglobinemia (pink to brown plasma), hemoglobinuria, and jaundice. Heinz bodies can be seen if red blood cells are stained using methyl violet.

Laboratory Analysis. Urine dipstick and hematocrit are simple and useful screening tools that can be done in the field. Hemoglobin (blood), bilirubin (urobilinogen), and protein should be monitored when using urine dipsticks to screen for hemolysis. It is important to differentiate the "blood" identified by urine dipstick as free hemoglobin or as red blood cells (hematuria). Hemoglobin in urine is present when red blood cells are destroyed in the hemolytic process, while intact red blood cells are present due to another pathologic process. Hematocrit testing, if performed, should be compared to baseline values. If facilities are available, other useful laboratory tests include blood and plasma hemoglobin levels, plasma haptoglobin level, reticulocyte count, lactose dehydrogenase level, and identification of Heinz bodies.

Primaquine Use in G-6-PD Deficient Personnel

G-6-PD Screening and Documentation. All Navy and Marine Corps personnel are tested for G-6-PD deficiency. Testing is qualitative, determining the presence of G-6-PD deficiency, but not the type or severity. Members who test positive must be informed of the deficiency, the signs and symptoms they may experience and why they may occur, and the risks of taking oxidant medications. They also should be advised to consult with their unit corpsman or medical officer if malaria medications are administered to them.

The results of G-6-PD screening must be recorded in individual medical records, along with an entry documenting individual counseling of their deficiency. Unit medical records should be checked periodically to ensure that G-6-PD and other important information such as immunization status, blood type, etc., are recorded. If the information is not available, testing should be repeated. Use of spreadsheet software and microcomputers is an excellent medium for maintenance of unit medical readiness data.

Current Navy policy prohibits primaquine prophylaxis of G-6-PD deficient service members. If, in the future, treatment of G-6-PD deficient personnel is authorized, testing for the specific type of deficiency is recommended. Once tested, such personnel should be informed of the type and details of their deficiency. If test information is not available as to an individual's specific type of deficiency when terminal primaquine prophylaxis is sanctioned, the dosage regimen should be given based on demographic data. These data support the assumptions that G-6-PD deficiency in Afro-American personnel is the G-6-PD^{A-} type, and personnel of European descent have the G-6-PD^{Med} type.

Terminal Primaquine Prophylaxis/Treatment. Primaquine remains the only drug available for treatment of the relapsing types of malaria. It can be used safely in G-6-PD deficient personnel under close medical supervision. Doses must be given less often and over a longer period of time to avoid a serious hemolytic reaction. Ensuring treatment compliance will be challenging, as the primaquine regimen consists of 24 doses over 8 weeks in G-6-PD^{A-} deficient personnel, and 60 doses over 30 weeks in G-6-PD^{Med} deficient personnel (see table 5-4).

Monitoring. If, in the future, primaquine prophylaxis of G-6-PD deficient personnel is authorized, monitoring of deficient members is recommended. G-6-PD deficient personnel taking primaquine should be advised to seek medical evaluation if any symptoms or change in urine color occur. A simple urine dipstick and/or hematocrit performed 3 to 4 days after the initial dose and checked periodically would identify severe cases of hemolysis.

Therapy of Drug Reaction. If hemolysis occurs, particularly in G-6-PD^{A-} deficient persons, transfusion is usually not required. Hemolytic episodes are usually self-limited, even if drug administration is continued. This is not the case with the more severe G-6-PD^{Med} deficiency and drug treatment should be stopped. If the rate of hemolysis is rapid, transfusion of whole blood or packed cells may be useful. Good urine flow should be maintained in patients with hemoglobinuria to prevent kidney damage. Folic acid may be beneficial as in other patients with increased bone marrow activity (an increase in bone marrow activity is caused by red blood cell formation).

Table 5-4. Primaquine Treatment Regimens

G-6-PD Normal	1 tablet* per day x 14 days
G-6-PD^{A-} Deficiency	3 tablets per week for 8 weeks
G-6-PD^{Med} Deficiency	2 tablets per week for 30 weeks

*1 tablet consists of 26.3 mg primaquine phosphate, 15 mg primaquine base.

CHAPTER SIX

MILITARY MALARIA CONTROL
RESPONSIBILITIES

Throughout history, diseases and non-battle injuries (DNBI) have resulted in more casualties to the Navy/Marine Corps team than combat. Historically, malaria has been the most formidable disease to prevent. The resources expended in its treatment, and the personnel hours lost due to malaria significantly decrease force readiness, especially in combat situations.

Prevention of DNBI is arguably the most important mission of military medicine. Success is achieved only when line commanders are convinced that principles of preventive medicine are an essential element in force protection. As Field Marshal Slim maintained (see Introduction), the countermeasures necessary to prevent malaria must be enforced by line commanders. Medical personnel must understand and practice the following three basic principles of Force Protection:

1) **Threat assessment.**
2) **Countermeasure selection and implementation.**
3) **Reassessment of threats and countermeasures guided by outcome measurement and analysis.**

After careful analysis of the deployment situation, appropriate countermeasure recommendations to commanders can be made. Then, with command support, countermeasure training and coordination can be instituted throughout the chain of command.

Medical Surveillance. Medical personnel must actively track unit illnesses and injuries. A single case of malaria may constitute an outbreak and signals a breakdown in preventive measures. Cases must be investigated and analyzed by unit medical personnel. Recommendations to correct the problem should be made immediately to the unit commander and followed by the institution of corrective measures.

This chapter will outline the application of the second and third principles to control malaria and other DNBIs by the chain of command. In general, malaria control is achieved through **Personal Protective Measures, Mosquito Control**, and **Chemoprophylaxis**. In military situations, personal protective measures and chemoprophylaxis are simple, effective, and successful. Mosquito control may be less suitable in contingency settings but can be particularly useful in long-term or humanitarian operations. Consult the cognizant medical entomologist. To prevent malaria, strong line involvement and enforcement is essential. Medical personnel must work closely with line commanders and staff to implement measures to prevent malaria.

I. Line Commander Responsibilities

CINCs and JTF Commanders. These commanders exercise authority over all assigned and attached forces in their area of operations. The decisions they make regarding medical guidance, assignment of medical tasks, and the joint medical concept of the operation are based on the advice received from CINC or Joint Task Force Surgeons. Prior to the operation, detailed medical guidance is published in Annex Q of the operation order. The malaria risk is characterized, and required countermeasures selected are included in that document. Annex Q is prepared by the CINC or JTF Surgeon staff, endorsed by the CINC or JTF commander.

This process reveals the impact that medical advice has on military operations. Line commanders need their medical officers to supply accurate, clear advice to enable them to make decisions to keep their forces ready. Jonathan Letterman, the Medical Director for the Army of the Potomac during the Civil War, clearly defines that role in the following quote:

> "A corps of medical officers was not established solely for the purpose of attending the sick and wounded...the labors of medical officers covers a more extended field. The leading idea, which should be constantly kept in view, is to strengthen the hands of the Commanding General by keeping his army in the most vigorous heal h, thus rendering it, in the highest degree, efficient for enduring fatigue and for figh ing. In this view, the duties of the corps are of vital importance to the success of an army, and commanders seldom appreciate the full affect of their proper fulfillment."

Fleet and Force Commanders. These service commands are responsible for training and equipping units in their service, and maintaining their operational readiness. In prevention of DNBI (malaria control), their function is to provide all supplies necessary for implementation of countermeasures, as well as to ensure that all personnel are trained to employ personal protective measures. An example of this is First Marine Expeditionary Force's readiness policy requiring every Marine deploying as part of a Marine Expeditionary Unit (MEU) to have three sets of utility uniforms pretreated with permethrin.

Unit Commanding Officers. The success of malaria control depends on the enforcement of personal protective measures by Commanding Officers (COs). Part of the responsibility of enforcing personal protective measures is ensuring that personnel are adequately trained and can employ them. Commanding Officers ultimately decide how chemoprophylaxis is administered, whether before a meal, by separate departments, or by employment of directly observed therapy (DOT). Finally, they must provide a surveillance report as directed in the Navy reportable disease instruction. Accurate surveillance data and analysis yield accurate reassessment of threats and countermeasures.

II. Medical Department Responsibilities

DNBI and malaria control efforts depend on medical department personnel. They provide the expertise to: 1) perform medical surveillance; 2) educate, train, and supervise the employment of personal protective measures and chemoprophylactic regimens; 3) diagnose and treat malaria, and other diseases and injuries; and 4) perform vector surveillance and control. Superior medical departments train their personnel to demonstrate and instruct other service members in the use of field hygiene and personal protective measures. In addition, they instruct corpsmen as well as medical officers to be familiar with the various chemoprophylaxis and treatment regimens, and the alternate treatments required for G-6-PD deficient individuals, pregnant service members, and persons who have had adverse reactions from anti-malarial drugs.

Medical personnel also must understand the threat in order to counter it. Essential sources of medical intelligence are the

Armed Forces Medical Intelligence Center, and Navy Environmental and Preventive Medicine Units. Appendix 1 describes in detail these and other resources from which medical intelligence, threat assessments, and other information can be obtained.

Senior Medical Officers. Force and Fleet medical officers have two priorities:

    1)   Advising force commanders of DNBI threats, including malaria, and recommending appropriate countermeasures.

    2)   Preparing medical department personnel to counter identified threats.

Advising force commanders of the appropriate countermeasures to employ requires medical commanders to characterize the DNBI threat. By combining medical intelligence on the area of operation with an understanding of mission operations, plans, and objectives, the risks to the force can be judged. Countermeasures are then recommended to reduce risks and ensure mission accomplishment. This is a synergistic process; countermeasures prevent illness and injury, increasing force readiness.

Part of the process of recommending countermeasures is estimating the resources needed to employ them. This includes identifying and directing necessary training, along with identifying and procuring necessary supplies needed to implement recommended countermeasures. This information needs to be passed on as expeditiously as possble to the personnel responsible for action.

Unit Medical Officers. Unit medical officers, including Independent Duty Corpsmen, are essential in prevention of DNBI and malaria. They advise their CO on all medical matters. Enforcement of personal protective measures and method of administration of chemoprophylaxis depend on the advice given the CO by the Unit medical officer. By doing continuous surveillance of malaria incidence rates, other DNBI rates, and proper employment of personal protective measures, Unit medical officers can monitor the success of countermeasures, and reassess the threats. Unit medical officers must also train and supervise the unit's corpsmen to ensure optimal medical care is delivered.

Flight Surgeons. Flight surgeon responsibility is the same as that of Unit medical officers, with special attention to the effects of malarial chemoprophylaxis medications on flight personnel. Continuous or periodic monitoring of flight personnel on medication may be required to ensure safety. Flight personnel under treatment for malaria cannot fly until completion of treatment and evaluation by a flight surgeon. It is important to note that chemoprophylaxis with mefloquine is not authorized for use in flight personnel.

Preventive Medicine Officers. The General Preventive Medicine Officer (PMO) serves as a source of information for all levels of the chain of command. Currently PMOs serve on all Marine Expeditionary Force staffs, and requests have been made to place PMOs on the staffs of the geographic CINCs. Knowledge of the general duties of all medical department personnel involved in malaria control (Medical Entomologists, Environmental Health Officers, Preventive Medicine Technicians) allows them to consult and coordinate the provision of any needed training, supplies, or control measures with units in the field or in garrison. PMOs will usually deploy to the area of operation with a deployable lab, a resource able to aid in disease diagnosis and vector identification and surveillance.

One of their primary duties is to coordinate or assist in any illness or outbreak investigation. All surveillance data are monitored and analyzed by PMOs, forwarded to all unit and military treatment facility medical departments, and to commanders, along with pertinent recommendations. Current malaria prevalence, incidence, and any pattern of drug resistance in an operational area are included in these reports. (Reports are not limited to malaria statistics).

Hospital Corpsmen. The training and support of hospital corpsmen is of paramount importance to force readiness and must be emphasized at every level in the chain of command. Hospital corpsmen are the first line of defense in malaria and DNBI prevention. Unit corpsmen perform most of the personal protective measures training given to unit personnel. They live among them in the field and monitor the daily employment of countermeasures. They supervise administration of chemoprophylaxis, and are often the first to initiate the diagnosis and care of any malaria cases.

Preventive Medicine Technicians (PMTs). These are specially trained hospital corpsman, and are directly involved in all aspects of malaria and DNBI control. They provide training in personal protective measures to hospital corpsmen and unit personnel. They also perform field vector surveillance, collect epidemiological data, and will supervise or conduct field sanitation and vector control measures if needed. They serve along side PMOs, and are excellent resources for preventive medicine information in the field.

Laboratory Personnel. Laboratory personnel assigned to deployable labs, fleet hospitals, Marine Medical Battalions, or any other unit that deploys to malaria endemic areas must be able to perform thick and thin peripheral blood smears and differentiate between the four plasmodia species that cause malaria in humans. They should be able to teach this diagnostic technique to interested medical personnel.

An important responsibility is sending prepared duplicate blood smear slides to the Navy Environmental and Preventive Medicine Unit assigned to monitor the area of operation. Such samples enable update of the area threat assessment and diagnosis confirmation. The slides should be both stained and unstained, and accompanied by identifying information and the clinical history of the case.

Environmental Health Officers (EHOs). Environmental Health Officers are often assigned to deployable labs, preventive medicine units, Marine Force Service Support Groups, Marine Divisions, Marine Air Wings, and Joint Task Forces. They assist in collection of epidemiological and entomological data, and evaluate the environmental conditions that affect malaria control. They also have a primary role in the training and supervision of PMTs.

Medical Entomologists. Medical entomologists obtain the most current mosquito information and recommend applicable methods of vector control. They supervise adult and larval mosquito surveys, pesticide application, and train personnel in identification and control measures. They are assigned to Marine Force Service Support Groups to:

1) Recommend and ensure that personal protective measures are employed.
2) Select optimum locations for bivouacs and base camps.
3) Recommend safe times for training and field exercises.

Preventive Medicine teams can deploy EHOs, Medical Entomologists, Epidemiologists, Laboratory Technicians, and Industrial Health Officers. These teams can provide varied and useful services to deployed forces.

III. Administrative Responsibilities

Medical Records. Medical records of Navy/Marine Corps service members are required to include:

G-6-PD Screening Results: A result, either deficient or normal, must be entered on a Standard Form 600 (SF 600). If deficient, this information must be highlighted on the Problem Summary List (NAVMED 6150/20). In addition, the "Sensitivities" block in the "Alert box" on the cover of their medical treatment record must be checked. Other health care beneficiaries, including civilian technical experts, should be offered this screening test if traveling to endemic areas.

Chemoprophylaxis. The date prophylaxis began and ended, drug type, and dosage should be entered on a SF 600. If terminal primaquine prophylaxis is given, entry of the same information is required.

All personnel required to take chemoprophylaxis must be informed of the reason for taking the medication, common side effects of the drug, and when to take the medication. It should also be communicated clearly that taking prophylactic medication does not guarantee malaria prevention.

Service members should be advised to seek medical evaluation if they suffer drug side effects or have symptoms of malaria. This information is usually presented at the unit level. When this information is presented, personal protective measures may be demonstrated, and DEET, permethrin, netting, and other necessary items may be issued.

Medical Event Reports. Medical Event Reports (MERs) are required, by instruction, on any member diagnosed with malaria. The report should be generated using the Naval Disease Reporting System software package which can be downloaded from the NEHC homepage (http://www-nehc.med.navy.mil). If the software is unavailable, a message can be generated. The MERs are then sent to the Navy Environmental and Preventive Medicine Unit assigned to monitor the area of operation. The message should also "info" all military treatment facilities in the area, the nearest Navy Disease Vector Ecology and Control Center, and the Navy Environmental Health Center (NEHC). The information is important to monitor and update both the malaria threat and presence of drug-resistant malaria in the area of operation.

The following is the minimum information included in the MER:

1) Patient travel history 3 months prior to diagnosis.
2) Type and duration of chemoprophylaxis or treatment medications taken, if applicable.
3) Interpretation (diagnosis) of blood smears performed on the patient.
4) Date that blood smears were sent to a Navy Environmental and Preventive Medicine Unit for confirmation.

Medical Treatment Facilities. The staff of Military Treatment Facilities that may receive malaria patients should be familiarized with treatment. Commanders should arrange training from available sources such as the Internal Medicine or Infectious Disease department, or the nearest Navy Environmental and Preventive Medicine Unit. A general in-service training session that includes the following topics is recommended:

1) Diagnosis, treatment and monitoring.
2) Common complications of severe falciparum malaria infections.
3) The physiology of terminal primaquine prophylaxis and G-6-PD deficiency.
4) Monitoring blood parasite concentration with peripheral blood smears for treatment response.

Another important aspect in the care of malaria patients is to send a timed and dated peripheral blood smear upon transfer, so the receiving facility can compare it with their initial blood smear, and confirm the diagnosis.

Medical Board Evaluations. Service members who develop severe malaria complicated by a severe hemolytic reaction characterized by hemoglobinuria together with the diagnosis of "blackwater fever" and/or renal failure are required to be evaluated for fitness for further duty by a Medical Board. A Medical Board is also required on personnel who develop a similar severe hemolytic reaction as a result of taking malaria chemoprophylactic drugs. The complication of cerebral malaria does not require evaluation by a Medical Board unless permanent neurologic disability has occurred.

Blood Donor Programs. Blood donation programs are subject to the guidance of BUMED P-5120, "Standards for Blood Bank and Transfusion Services." The directive is applicable to both military and civilian blood banks and requires that individuals treated for malaria wait three years from the date of completion of therapy to donate blood. Individuals who took malaria chemoprophylactic drugs while in endemic areas must also wait three years from completion of chemoprophylaxis to donate blood. The reason for the waiting period is to prevent donated blood from being contaminated by malaria parasites, not drugs.

Individuals who visited a malaria-endemic area without taking chemoprophylactic drugs and remained asymptomatic are required to wait 6 months before being eligible to donate blood. Persons placed on chemoprophylactic therapy in readiness, but who did not travel into a malaria endemic area, do not have a required waiting period to donate blood.

APPENDIX ONE

INFORMATION & INTELLIGENCE SOURCES; CONSULTANTS

Introduction. Resources listed in this appendix for malaria and DNBI prevention are divided into two general sections, Medical Information and Medical Intelligence. Directions on how to acquire information, references, or software are included along with points of contact and Internet/E-mail addresses. Some of the Medical Intelligence products listed are classified and require a security clearance for access.

I. MEDICAL INFORMATION

1. Military Sources

A. General Policy and Guidance

- Bureau of Medicine and Surgery
  Division of Occupational and Preventive Medicine
  (MED-24B) 2300 E Street NW
  Washington, DC 20372-5300
  Phone: (202) 762-3495; DSN: 294-3495;
  FAX: (202) 762-3490

- Navy Environmental Health Center
  Preventive Medicine Directorate
  2510 Walmer Ave
  Norfolk, VA 23513-2617
  Phone: (757) 462-5593; DSN: 253-5593
  FAX: (757) 444-9691, DSN 564-
  E-mail: prevmed@med.navy.mil

B. Navy Environmental & Preventive Medicine Units (NEPMUs), four world-wide:

- **Navy Environmental & Preventive Medicine Unit 2**
  Epidemiology Department, Norfo k, VA
  Phone: (757) 444-7671; DSN 564-
  Fax: (757) 444-1191; DSN 564-
  E-mail: epi-nepmu2-nor@nepmu2.med.navy.mil

- **Navy Environmental & Preventive Medicine Unit 5**
  Epidemiology Department, San Diego, CA
  Phone: (619) 556-7070; DSN 526-
  Fax: (619) 556-7071; DSN 526-7071;
  E-mail: nepmu5@nepmu5.med.navy.mil

- **Navy Environmental & Preventive Medicine Unit 6**
  Epidemiology Department, Pearl Harbor, HI
  Phone: (808) 473-0555; DSN 315-
  Fax: (808) 473-9361; DSN 315-
  E-mail: nepmu6@nepmu6.med.navy.mil

- **Navy Environmental & Preventive Medicine Unit 7**
  Epidemiology Department, Sigonella NAS, Sicily, Italy
  Phone: From US 011-39-095-56-3781;
  From Italy 095-56-3781;
  From Europe 0039-095-56-3781; DSN 624-3781
  Fax: from US 011-39-095-56-4100; DSN 624-4100
  E-mail: sig1pmu@sig10.med.navy.mil

⇒ **NEPMUs Publications and Services available:**
  * Pre-deployment medical briefings.
  * Courses on malaria, hepatitis, field sanitation, etc.
  * Consultation with representative of Epidemiology Department.
  * PPM – Entomologist.

C. Navy Disease Vector Ecology and Control Centers (DVECCs), two within CONUS:

- **DVECC, Jacksonville**: P.O. Box 43, Bldg. 937, Naval Air Station Jacksonville, FL 32212-0043 (904) 542-2424; DSN 942-
  E-mail: dvj0ccj@jax10.med.navy.mil

- **DVECC, Bangor**: 19950 Seventh Ave. Poulsbo, WA 98370-7405 (360) 315-4450; DSN 322-   E-mail:postmaster@ndvecc.navy.mil
⇒ **DVECC Publications and services available:**
  * "VECTRAPS," or vector reports, descriptions of disease vectors and control measures worldwide.
  * Information on pesticide usage and resistance and personal protective measures.

D. Navy Infectious Diseases Consultants

- National Naval Medical Center
  Infectious Diseases Division
  8901 Wisconsin Ave
  Bethesda, MD 20889-5600
  DSN: 295-4237
  Phone: (301) 295-4237
  Fax: -2831
- Naval Medical Center
  Infectious Diseases Division
  620 John Paul Jones Circle
  Portsmouth, VA 23708
  Phone: (757) 953-5179
  Fax: -7674
- Naval Medical Center
  Infectious Diseases Division
  34800 Bob Wilson Drive Suite 201
  San Diego, CA 92134-1201
  DSN: 522-7475
  Phone: (619) 532-7475
  Fax: -7478/8798

E. Naval Medical Research Units

- Naval Medical Research Institute
  Director for Malaria Programs
  12300 Washington Ave
  Rockville, MD 20852
  Phone: (202) 295-2079; DSN 295-2079;
  Fax: (202) 295-6171
  E-mail: hoffmans@nmripo.nmri.nnmc.navy.mil

- U.S. Naval Medical Research Institute No. 3
  PSC 452, Box 5000 FPO AE 09835-0007
  (Cairo, Egypt)
  Phone: ask overseas operator for Cairo, 820727

- U.S. Naval Medical Research Institute No. 2
  Box 3, APO AP 96520
  (Jakarta, Indonesia)
  Phone: ask overseas operator for Jakarta, 414-507

- U.S. Naval Medical Research Institute Detachment
  American embassy Unit 3800, APO AA 34031-0008
  (Lima, Peru)
  Phone: ask overseas operator for Lima, 52-1560, 9662
  Within U.S.: 011-51-14-52-1562, 9662

F. Walter Reed Army Institute of Research

- Division of Preventive Medicine (202) 782-1334; DSN 662-
- Travel Medicine Clinic (202) 782-1302/1312; DSN 662-

G. Preventive Medicine Recommendations for specific operations

- Available from the JTF or CINC Surgeon's office, Fleet or Force Surgeon's office, or the Navy Environmental and Preventive Medicine Unit assigned to the area of operation.
- If involved in the planning phase for a regularly recurring exercise, contact the cognizant NEPMU to obtain recommendations for specific operation.

H. Armed Forces Medical Intelligence Center. See Medical Intelligence section for description of AFMIC products including the Medical Environmental Disease Intelligence and Countermeasures CD-ROM ("MEDIC").

2. Civilian Sources

A. Sources for Individual Travelers. These are commercial, computer-based, medically oriented travel risk information and recommendation services which are updated regularly.

- Travax™ Shoreland, Inc. P.O. Box 13795 Milwaukee, WI, 53213-0795; (800) 755-2301; (414) 774-4600; Fax-4060

- Travel Care™, Care Ware, Inc. 9559 Poole Street, La Jolla, CA, 92037; (619) 455-1484; Fax -5429
- Centers for Disease Control and Prevention: Fax Information Service for International Travel. To receive a document call (404) 332-4565, and follow the prompts. To get a directory, call the fax number and enter "document number 000005" when prompted by the voice menu. This service is available year round, 24 hours a day.

B. Internet Homepages And Other Computer Related Sources:

- NEHC Web page: *http://www-nehc.med.navy.mil/*
- CDC: http://www.cdc.gov/travel/
- American Society of Tropical Medicine and Hygiene (ASTMH): http://www.ASTMH.org/
- PROMED: Intended to be an increasingly sensitive aid for detection of outbreaks worldwide: *http://www.fas.org /promed/*
- Medical Matrix: Huge database listing hundreds of Internet available information sources: *http://www.slackinc.com/ matrix/*
- Shoreland Travel Health Information Service: *http//www.shoreland.com*
- National L brary of Medicine: *http://www.ncbi.nlm.nih.gov/PubMed*
- Rollins School of Medicine at Emory University, Public Health Resources on the web: http://www.sph.emory.edu/PHIL/

3. Textbooks and Publications

A) *Medical Products for Supporting Military Readiness: Vaccines & Drugs* **("The GO Book"),** Nov 1996, U.S. Army Medical Research & Materiel Command: Secretary of the General Staff, USA-MC, Fort Detrick, Maryland, (301) 619-7111, DSN: 343-

B) *Pocket Book of Infectious Disease Therapy,* Bartlett JG, Williams & Wilkins, 1996

C) *Control of Communicable Diseases Manual,* Chin, ed., American Public Health Association, 17th Edition, 2000

D) **Hunter's** *Tropical Medicine,* Strickland, ed., Saunders, 7th Edition, 1991

e) ***Principles and Practice of Infectious Diseases***, Mandell et. al., Churchill Livingstone, 4th Edition, 1995

F) ***Manson's Tropical Diseases,*** Cook, ed., Saunders, 1996

G) ***Wilderness Medicine,*** Auerbach, ed., Mosby, 1995

H) ***The Sanford Guide to Antimicrobial Therapy,*** Sanford, ed., Antimicrobial Therapy, Inc., yearly

II. MEDICAL INTELLIGENCE

A. AFMIC. The primary source of medical intelligence products is the Armed Forces Medical Intelligence Center (AFMIC), a division of the Defense Intelligence Agency, located at Fort Detrick, Maryland. Described are the medical intelligence products AFMIC provides:

- **Medical Environmental Disease Intelligence and Countermeasures CD-ROM ("MEDIC").** "MEDIC" provides worldwide disease and environmental health risks hyperlinked to Joint Service approved country-specific countermeasure recommendations and other pertinent military medical references. Also included in "MEDIC" are military and civilian health care delivery capabilities, operational information, arthropod vector information, an expanded poisonous snake section on some countries, an expanded section on poisonous and injurious plants, and significant portions of *Control of Communicable Diseases Manual* (included by permission from the American Public Health Association).

- **Infectious Disease Risk Assessment, (IDRA) and Environmental Health Risk Assessment, (EHRA).** Infectious Disease and Environmental Health Risk Assessments are unclassified risk assessments on individual countries without *countermeasure recommendations*. They are available in three media: by message, via the AFMIC bulletin board system (BBS), and on the "MEDIC" CD-ROM. The most current assessments are available through the BBS, and each month some countries are updated through a cyclic update process. Assessments are oriented for and available only to operational U.S. military personnel. IDRAs and EHRAs were formerly known as the Disease and Environmental Alert Reports (DEARs).

- **Disease Occurrence Worldwide (DOWW).** Classified and unclassified supplements to IDRAs and EHRAs. The DOWW is a monthly compilation of reports on disease outbreaks which serve as late-breaking updates to the IDRA. DOWW is published as an unclassified message with a classified supplement if necessary.
- **AFMIC Wire.** A bi-weekly message serving as an update of infectious disease and environmental risks worldwide. AFMIC's version of Headline News, it is a current intelligence document, which presents analysis of new information of potential tactical interest. In addition to the scheduled wire, "Special Wires" may be produced periodically on topics of interest to deploying units.
- **Medical Capability Studies (MEDCAP).** Information on foreign country assets and medical infrastructure. It evaluates the ability of a country to support its armed forces in peace and war, and the suitability of facilities in the country to support U.S. operations. These studies are produced on countries of tactical significance, usually those with power projection capability.
- **Health Services Assessment (HSA).** Health Service Assessments are comprehensive evaluations of a country's health infrastructure, and may be considered a short form of the MEDCAP. HSA evaluates a country in less detail, and is designed to provide an overview of a country's civilian and military/health care systems to support operational planning.
- **Urban Area Medical Capabilities Study.** The Urban Study was recently redesigned to meet the needs of United States Special Operations Command (USSOCOM). It includes a map of the urban area, general health information, and locations, descriptions, and photographs of key medical treatment facilities.
- **AFMIC Bulletin Board System (BBS).** The BBS is an automated on-line system for the dissemination of unclassified medical intelligence products. This system is designed to provide timely, user friendly access to finished AFMIC products. All textual components of the "MEDIC"

are available on the BBS. The BBS System Operator may be reached at (301) 619-2686 or DSN 343-2686. The BBS may be accessed by dialing: (301) 619-3625 or 2000 or DSN 343-3625 or 2000.

- **Request for Information (RFIs).** An RFI is a way to ask AFMIC for answers to questions not found in published studies, usually requiring AFMIC to assemble specific information. The RFI system is designed to respond to requests for specific information on countries or areas worldwide, 24 hours per day, 7 days per week. RFIs should be directed to AFMIC through unit intelligence sections by way of the Community On-line Intelligence System for End-Users and Managers (COLISEUM) or by contacting AFMIC Operations at their 24 hour contact number, (301) 619-7574 or DSN 343-7574. Their phones are secure via STU-III through the TS-SCI level.

Procedures for obtaining the AFMIC wire, the DOWW, the IDRA, and the EHRA. AFMIC produces the AFMIC Wire under Address Indicator Group (AIG) 6623 for CONUS plus Alaska & Hawaii, and under AIG 12630 for OCONUS not including Alaska & Hawaii. The DOWW, IDRA, and EHRA are transmitted under AIG 12243 for CONUS plus Alaska & Hawaii and AIG 11829 for OCONUS not including Alaska & Hawaii. To be added to distribution for any of the AFMIC message products, please send name, organization, mailing address, routing indicator, plain language address, DSN and commercial telephone numbers, and a brief justification to:

AFMIC
ATTN: MA-1
Frederick, MD 21702-5004
or
DIRAFMIC FT DETRICK MD//MA-1

AFMIC can be reached at (301) 619-3837 or DSN 343-3837 for information.

⇒ **Procedures for receiving hardcopy AFMIC products and other intelligence products.** Hardcopy publications produced by AFMIC are disseminated by the Defense Intelligence Agency through the Defense Intelligence

Dissemination System (DIDS). An organization receives products based on requirements registered by the organization's Intelligence Office (IN) in a Statement of Intelligence Interest (SII). Largely, the SII is maintained by the IN or Security Office. Once a document is published by AFMIC, it is automatically mailed to the organization's IN or Security Office for distribution within the organization.

Once an organization has an SII registered distribution for AFMIC hardcopy products, but is not receiving some publications, its IN can modify the SII by adding the desired Intelligence Function Codes (IFCs) and country codes for those publications.

If an organization does not have an SII registered with DIA, follow the procedures as outlined in DIA Regulation No. 59-1, dated 12 June 1995, "DoD Intelligence Dissemination Program."

B. CIA World Factbook. The CIA World Factbook is an unclassified publication that provides general political and economic data on all countries of the world. It is updated annually and available as a hardcopy publication or through the Internet CIA home page. There is also a classified supplement that provides information on military, security, and intelligence forces worldwide.

C. Military Capabilities Study (MCS). The MCS is designed to serve as a ready reference document for national, operational, and tactical planners and consumers. Each study presents a compilation of intelligence on forces and resources that contr bute to the military security of each country, and on the political and economic factors affecting the country's military capabilities.

D. Intelink. This is the classified Internet system, and functions in the same manner as Netscape[R] or Internet Exchange[R], and documents can be easily downloaded and printed. Within the intelligence community it is rapidly becoming the preferred method of dissemination of information.

The ultimate goal is to have INTELINK available to all battalion level and higher intelligence sections. National level intelligence organizations, including each of the Unified Command Joint Intelligence Centers and AFMIC have home pages on INTELINK. All AFMIC products, and most recent intelligence publications, may be found there.

E. **Internet Sites.** There are a number of unclassified sources available. The Central Intelligence Agency has a home page where users may access the World Factbook. The State Department home page contains State Department country fact sheets, embassy information, and travel advisories. Other commercial databases are available which address travel medicine. Take time to find and bookmark useful resources.

F. **Joint Worldwide Intelligence Communication System (JWICS).** This secure telecommunications system links sites throughout the intelligence and operations communities, and allows secure teleconferencing. In support of time sensitive or complex requirements, it may be poss ble to arrange a teleconference between medical planners and AFMIC analysts. To arrange a conference, contact the unit intelligence officer to determine if a JWICS site exists and is available, then work with the local site manager and AFMIC Operations on specifics.

APPENDIX TWO

MOSQUITO VECTORS AND IDENTIFICATION

Introduction. Human malaria is transmitted only by mosquitoes belonging to the genus *Anopheles*. Currently 422 species of *Anopheles* mosquitoes have been identified throughout the world, 70 of which transmit malaria. Of the 70 species that transmit malaria, only 40 are of major significance.

Anopheles mosquitoes are most frequently found in tropical regions, but are also found in temperate climates and in the Arctic during summer (see Appendix Table 2.1). As a rule, they are not found at elevations above 2000-2500 meters (6500-8200 ft).

Mosquito Life Cycle. Development time from egg to adult depends on species and temperature, ranging from 7 days at an average temperature of $31^{o}C$, to 20 days at an average temperature of $20^{o}C$. Life span is species specific, and is affected by temperature, humidity, and presence of natural enemies. When the temperature is over $35^{o}C$ or the humidity is less than 50%, longevity is greatly reduced. Average life span of a female mosquito under favorable conditions is 10-14 days, with some able to live as long as 3-4 weeks.

Eggs. Females lay their first batch of eggs 3-6 days after they emerge from the pupal stage. Anopheline eggs are laid singly on the type of water preferred by the particular species. They are blackish, 0.5 mm long, and have tiny air-filled floats that let them drift on the water surface. Eggs hatch 2-3 days after being laid.

Larvae. *Anopheles* mosquito larvae have unique characteristics. They lack the prominent air tube or siphon found in other mosquito species larvae. They float horizontally on the surface of the water, and turn their heads 180° to feed. They move in sudden jerks, and sink below the surface if disturbed. After molting three times, they develop into pupae.

Appendix Figure 2-1. Differences between *Anopheles*, *Aedes*, and *Culex* mosquitoes at various stages of development.

| | **Anophelines** *Anopheles* | **Culicines** | |
		Aedes	*Culex*
Eggs	with floats, laid singly on water	no floats, laid singly on dry/ damp surface	no floats, laid in rafts on water
Larva	no air tube rest parallel to water surface, head rotated 180° when feeding	one tuft on short stout air tube rest at angle to surface, head not rotated	several tufts on slender air tube rest at angle to surface, head not rotated
Adult	resting position	resting position	resting position

Pupae. Mosquito pupae are comma-shaped. There are two separate body regions: the cephalothorax (the head and thorax combined), and the abdomen (tail section). They do not feed, but come to the water surface to breathe through short paired respiratory trumpets. The pupal stage lasts 2-4 days, after which an adult mosquito emerges.

Adults. In order for eggs to develop, female mosquitoes require at least one, sometimes two blood meals. Male mosquitoes do not take a blood meal. Adult mosquitoes typically fly and bite within a two-three kilometer radius of breeding areas but strong winds have carried them as far as 30km. Peak biting time is between 1900-2100 hours for some species while other species such as *A. gambiae* are late feeders, biting between 2400-0300 hours. Control methods should be targeted to coincide with peak biting times when possible. The resting posture of adult mosquitoes differs by species (see Appendix Figure 2-1).

Appendix Table 2-1. *Anopheles* species of importance in transmission of human malaria.

Region	Description	Major Vectors
North America	From Great Lakes to southern Mexico	*A. freeborni* *A. quadrimaculatus* *A. hermsi*
Central America	Southern Mexico, Caribbean islands, fringe of South American coast	*A. albimanus* *A. argyritarsis* *A. pseudopunctipennis* *A. aquasalis* *A. darlingi*
South America	South American continent	*A. pseudopunctipennis* *A. punctimacula* *A. albimanus* *A. albitaris* *A. aquasalis* *A. darlingi*
North Eurasia	Europe and west Asia, Arctic south excluding Mediterranean coast	*A. atroparvus*

Appendix Table 2-1, continued. *Anopheles* species of importance in transmission of human malaria.

Region	Description	Major Vectors
Mediterranean	South coast of Europe, North coast of Africa	*A. atroparvus* *A. labranchiae* *A. sacharovi* *A. superpictus*
Africa-Arabia	Saharan Africa, North Arabian peninsula	*A. pharoensis* *A. sergentii*
Sub-Saharan Africa	South Arabian peninsula, Ethiopia, Somalia, tropical Africa, Madagascar	*A. funestus* *A. arabiensis* *A. gambiae* *A. melas* *A. merus*
India-Iran	Northwest of the Persian Gulf, Indian subcontinent	*A. culicifacies* *A. fluviatilis*
Indochina	Indochinese peninsula	*A. dirus* *A. maculatus* *A. fluviatilis* *A. minimus*

Appendix Table 2-1, continued. *Anopheles* species of importance in transmission of human malaria.

Region	Description	Major Vectors
Malaysia	Indonesia, Malaysian peninsula, Philippines, Timor	*A. campestris* *A. donaldi* *A. letifer* *A. aconitus* *A. balabacensis* *A. dirus* *A. flavirostris* *A. leucosphyrus* *A. maculatus* *A. sundaicus*
China	Korea, Taiwan, Japan, and the Coast of mainland China	*A. anthropophagus* *A. sinensis*
Australia-Pacific	Northern Australia, Papua New Guinea, islands west of 175° east latitude	*A. farauti type 1* *A. farauti type 2* *A. koliensis* *A. punctulatus*

APPENDIX THREE

LABORATORY DIAGNOSTIC TECHNIQUES

Introduction. Despite development of serological techniques, conclusive diagnosis of malaria continues to be made through microscopic examination of peripheral blood smears. This is the only method that can differentiate among the four species of plasmodia that cause human malaria.

> **Thick Smears.** Red blood cells are hemolyzed in thick smears; leukocytes and any malaria parasites present are the detectable elements. The hemolysis and slow drying that occur in thick smear preparation cause distortion of plasmodia morphology, making differentiation of species difficult. Thick smears are used to detect infection, and estimate parasite concentration.

> **Thin Smears.** Thin smears are fixed with methanol, preventing hemolysis. Red blood cells are intact, and any *Plasmodia* present are less likely to be distorted, and remain within erythrocytes. Identification of specific species is usually done using thin smears after detection of parasites on the thick smears.

Navy Environmental & Preventive Medicine Units offer training classes on preparation of thick and thin smears and microscopic examination for diagnosis of malaria. This appendix summarizes thick and thin blood smear preparation for field reference.

Drawing Blood

- Anytime malaria is suspected.
- Repeat if smears are negative.
- Maximum frequency: once per hour.

Obtaining Blood

- Fresh blood is required from either fingerstick or venous phlebotomy

- Follow universal precautions (gloves, hand washing, proper handling and disposal of sharp instruments and other materials contaminated with blood)
- Fingerstick Method:
  1) Clean end of finger with disinfectant solution.
  2) Wipe fingertip with sterile material (remove remaining disinfectant that may interfere with diagnostic process).
  3) Pierce fingertip with sterile lancet.
  4) Allow blood to flow freely, do not squeeze finger.
- For venous blood obtained in a vacutainer, use a pipette to apply a drop of blood to slide(s) for thick and thin smears

Slide Preparation (see Appendix Figure 3-1)

⇒ **Thick Smear**

  5) Wipe away first drop of blood at fingerstick site. Then touch a clean microscope slide near one end to the next blood drop that forms.
  6) Spread drop of blood with corner of another slide to make an area about 1 cm in diameter.
- This is the thick smear. Correct thickness is attained when newsprint is barely legible through the smear.

⇒ **Thin Smear**

  7) Touch a new drop of blood (smaller than the first) with the edge of a clean slide.
  8) Bring the edge of the slide with the new drop of blood to the surface of the first slide. Place it at the far end, and wait until the blood spreads along the whole edge.
  9) Holding the slide at an angle of 45^0, push it forward with a rapid, gentle movement.
- For preparation of separate slides for thick and thin smears, use a second slide in step 4.
- Dry the smears. Air dry, allowing 10 minutes for the thin smear and 30 minutes for the thick smear.
- Mark slide with patient identification and date and time of collection. This can be done using a pencil on the thin smear after it has dried.

Fixing Thin Smears

- After drying, only thin smears are fixed. Fixing is done using methanol in one of two ways:

  10) Dip thin smear into methanol for 5 seconds.

  11) Dab thin smear with methanol-soaked cotton ball.

- Do not fix the thick smear. Even exposure of the thick smear to methanol fumes will prevent hemolysis and make it unreadable. If using the one slide method, prevent exposure of the thick smear to methanol or methanol fumes by carefully dipping or dabbing the slide, and gently blowing the fumes away from the thick smear area.

Staining Slides

Giemsa stain is available in the military supply system, and this staining method is presented. Preparation of Giemsa staining solution is done with buffered water and Giemsa concentrate. Do not shake the Giemsa concentrate as this will cause suspension of particulate matter in the stain resulting in artifacts on final slides. Formation of artifacts renders slides difficult to interpret.

Preparation of Giemsa staining solution

1) Prepare buffered water solution, **pH 7.2:**
   - Mix capful of buffering salts into 1000 ml of distilled water.
   - Check pH. Titrate with sodium hydroxide (NaOH) solution until pH is 7.2.

Appendix Figure 3-1. Thick and Thin Blood Smear Preparation.

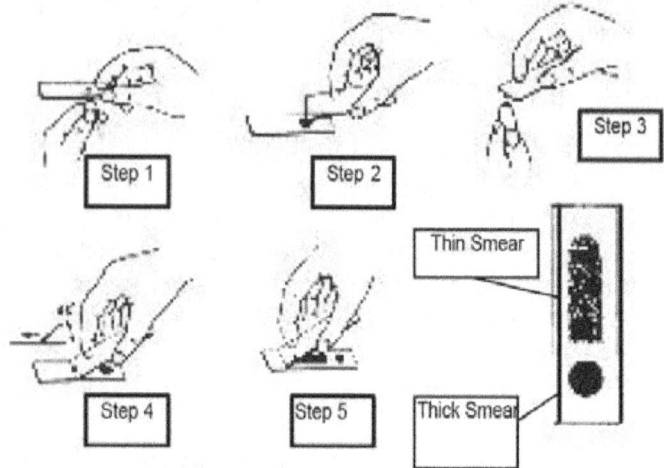

2) Prepare Giemsa staining solution by mixing:
   - 1 part **unshaken** Giemsa stain concentrate.
   - 9 parts buffered water.

Slide Staining with prepared Giemsa solution

- Place slides flat in a staining rack or other suitable surface.
- Cover with 1-2 ml of Giemsa solution.
- Let stand for 10 minutes.
- Gently rinse by "floating" excess stain off slide with buffered water; be careful not to wash the blood smear away.
- Rinse until no more stain is seen in solution.
- Dry smear side down, making sure that smear does not touch the slide rack or other surface used for drying.

Slide Preparation Pointers

- Clean microscope slides before use. Blood will spread cleanly, stain will adhere properly, and no artifacts will impede diagnosis.
- Do not fix slides with a heat source. If overexposed to heat, parasites are destroyed, and cannot be seen microscopically.
- Parasites stain best at pH of 7.2. Check stain pH for optimal staining.
- Filter the Giemsa stain. Removal of particles and residue will make slides much easier to interpret.

Microscopic Examination of Thick and Thin Blood Smears

Training and experience are essential for accurate reading. Slides should be examined for at least 20 minutes before being judged to be free of malaria parasites. Parasites are often not readily apparent, and quick visual scans are insufficient for diagnostic purposes. Appendix Table 3-1 shows selected microscopic characteristics of human malaria species.

Part of the diagnostic process is estimation of the extent of infection. Two methods are presented to estimate the parasite concentration or parasitemia. One requires the use of thick smears, and is called the **Absolute Numbers Method**. The other requires the use of thin smears, and is called the **Percent Method.**

Absolute Numbers Method (thick smear)

This method is based on the assumption that 8000 leukocytes (white blood cells) are found in a ml of blood. By counting the number of parasites seen in same visual fields needed to count either 200 or 500 leukocytes, the parasite concentration per ml can be estimated. Perform the following steps to estimate parasite concentration:

1) Examine the equivalent of 0.25 ml of blood (100 visual fields using a 7X ocular lens and a 100X oil-immersion objective lens) to determine if an infection exists.
2) In a systematic manner of scanning visual fields, identify 200 leukocytes, while counting the number of malarial parasites in those same visual fields.
3) If after 200 leukocytes have been identified and less than 9 malarial parasites have been counted, continue the process until 500 leukocytes have been identified.
4) If after 200 leukocytes have been identified and 10 or more parasites have been counted, record the number of parasites counted per 200 leukocytes.

Appendix Table 3-1. Selected microscopic characteristics

Species	Stages found in circulating Blood	Appearance of Red Blood Cells	
		Size	Stippling
Plasmodium falciparum	Trophozoites Gametocytes	Normal	Maurer's dots or clefts infrequently seen
Plasmodium vivax	All: Schizonts Trophozoites Gametocytes	Enlarged, Maximum size may be 1.5-2 times normal	Schuffner's dots may be present
Plasmodium ovale	All: Schizonts Trophozoites Gametocytes	Enlarged, Maximum size may be 1.25-1.5 times normal	Schuffner's dots may be present
Plasmodium malariae	All: Schizonts Trophozoites Gametocytes	Normal	Ziemann's dots rarely seen

5) Once 500 leukocytes have been identified, record the number of parasites counted.

6) Convert the parasite count per leukocytes identified into parasite concentration per ml with one of the following formulas:

$$\frac{\text{Number of parasites} \times 8000}{\text{Number of leukocytes counted}} = \text{parasites per ml}$$

or

if 200 leukocytes were counted:

$$\text{Number of parasites counted} \times 40 = \text{parasites per ml}$$

or

if 500 leukocytes were counted:

$$\text{Number of parasites counted} \times 16 = \text{parasites per ml}$$

Appendix Table 3-1. Selected microscopic characteristics (con't)

Appearance of Parasites		
Cytoplasm	Pigment	No. of merozoites
Double dots in rings common, rings small and delicate	Black Coarse and conspicuous in gametocytes	6-32 Avg. = 10-24
Ameboid trophs light blue, has irregular "spread out" appearance in troph stage	Golden-brown, inconspicuous	12-24 Avg. = 16
Rounded, compact trophs, dark to medium blue, usually dense; Chromatin is large	Dark brown, conspicuous	6-14 Avg. = 8
Rounded, compact trophs, dark blue with dense cytoplasm; band form trophs occasionally seen	Dark brown, coarse, conspicuous	6-12 Avg. = 8 "Rosette" occasionally seen

7) All parasite species and forms are tabulated together. This includes both sexual (gametocytes) and asexual (trophozoites, merozoites) forms.

Percent Method (thin smear).

This method estimates the percentage of red blood cells infected with malarial parasites. It is based on the number of red blood cells found parasitized on a thin smear, and is executed in the following manner:

1) Locate an area in the thin smear where red blood cells are close together but not touching.
2) Scan in a systematic method (use the microscope stage control to scan one "row" at a time).

3) Count the total number of red blood cells in each row. At the same time, tabulate the number of red blood cells parasitized.
4) Count a total of 300-500 red blood cells.
5) Divide the number parasitized by the total number counted and multiply the result by 100 to obtain a percentage estimate of red blood cells parasitized:

$$\frac{\text{Red Blood Cells parasitized}}{\text{Total Red Blood Cells counted}} \times 100 = \text{Percent of Red Blood Cells parasitized}$$

6) If occasional parasites are seen when scanning the smear, but none are identified during the process of counting 300-500 red blood cells, a percentage value of less than 1% of red blood cells parasitized is assigned.
7) An estimate of less than 1% of red blood cells parasitized does not need to be refined, since no clinical predictive value is gained. It is values of 2-3% or above that are of clinical concern.

Future Diagnostic Techniques

New, easy to perform serum serology techniques for malaria diagnosis are being developed. Two such methods, now approved by the FDA (*Para*Sight[R]F, Becton Dickinson, Sparks, MD; ICT Malaria P.f[R], ICT Diagnostics, Sydney, Australia), are designed for easy performance in field situations, and require no laboratory experience and little training. Both tools detect *P. falciparum* serologically using enzyme linked immunosorbent assay (ELISA), with results in 10 minutes. Clinical trials show these methods detect *P. falciparum* infections at parasite blood concentration of greater than 40 parasites per microliter (>40 parasites/µl).

APPENDIX FOUR

ANTIMALARIAL MEDICATIONS

Antimalarial drugs are divided into 4 classifications corresponding to their action on the different plasmodium life cycle stages in human hosts (see Table 5-1). The 4 classes are listed below:

1) Blood schizonticides attack plasmodia in red blood cells preventing or terminating the clinical attack.
2) Tissue schizonticides attack the exoerythrocytic forms in the liver.
3) Gametocytocidal drugs attack the gametocyte stage in red blood cells.
4) Hypnozoiticidal drugs kill dormant *P. vivax* or *P. ovale* hypnozoites in liver cells.

All common drugs used worldwide for treatment of malaria are discussed in this chapter. As with treatment of tuberculosis, multi-drug treatment regimens are becoming necessary as drug-resistant strains emerge. The status, availability, effectiveness, dosage, and side effects of each are presented. Drugs are listed by generic name in alphabetical order and divided into three sections; 1) anti-malarial drugs available

Table 5-1. Antimalarial Drugs classified by action on *Plasmodia* Life Cycle Stages

Drug Class	Drugs
Blood Schizontocide	Chloroquine, Quinine, Quinidine, Mefloquine, Halofantrine, Sulfonamides, Tetracyclines, Atovaquone, Artemisinin compounds
Tissue Schizontocide	Primaquine, Proguanil, Pyrimethamine,
Gametocidal	Primaquine
Hypnozoitocidal	Primaquine

through the military supply system; 2) Anti-malarial drugs available in the U.S., but not in the military supply system; and 3) Anti-malarial drugs under development or available in foreign countries. An important avenue of treatment is nasogastric administration of oral anti-malarial medications. If intravenous treatment in severe malaria patients is not possible, oral anti-malarial medications pulverized, mixed with water, and delivered via nasogastric tube are absorbed well and effectively. Dosage for nasogastric treatment is the same as the oral dose.

Section 1. Antimalarial Drugs Available in the Military Supply System

Chloroquine Phosphate

Status: FDA approved.

Availability: Currently available.

Product: A 4-aminoquinoline compound, chloroquine is a blood schizonticide active against *P. vivax, P. malariae,* and *P. ovale.* It has limited activity against most *P. falciparum* infections.

Description: 500 mg (300 mg base) tablets for oral administration.

Effectiveness: Chloroquine phosphate is indicated for suppressive treatment and for acute attacks of malaria due to *Plasmodium vivax, P. malariae, P. ovale,* and susceptible strains of *P. falciparum.* It does not prevent relapse in patients with *P. vivax* and *P. ovale* infections, because it does not eliminate persistent liver stage parasites. Primaquine must be given to achieve radical cure (elimination of dormant hypnozoites in liver cells). Because of the increasing frequency of parasite resistance to chloroquine, its use as a prophylactic is limited to Mexico, Central America, and limited areas of the Middle East.

Dose & Administration: For prophylaxis: One 500 mg tablet weekly beginning 2 weeks prior to departure to endemic areas and continued for 4 additional weeks upon return.

For treatment: An initial dose of two 500 mg tablets followed by one 500 mg tablet in 6-8 hours, then a single 500 mg dose on each of two consecutive days for a total of five tablets (2,500 mg) in 3 days.

Side Effects: The most frequently observed side effects are gastrointestinal and include anorexia, nausea, vomiting, diarrhea, and abdominal cramps. Mild and transient headache, tinnitus, and deafness have been reported. Ocular reactions including blurred vision, and reversible interference with visual accommodation or focusing of vision may also occur. Long-term or high-dosage therapy may result in irreversible retinal damage.

Chloroquine may cause hemolysis when administered to patients with G-6-PD deficiency, but reactions are not as severe as those seen with primaquine. G-6-PD deficient service members taking chloroquine prophylaxis should be informed of side effects (see Chapter 6), and advised to seek medical evaluation if they occur. For severe reactions, an alternate prophylactic regimen should be provided.

Doxycycline Hyclate

Availability: Currently available.
Product: A widely used antibiotic useful as an anti-malarial primarily for prevention of *P. falciparum* infections.
Description: Available as 100mg tablets for oral administration.
Effectiveness: Doxycycline is indicated for the prophylaxis of malaria due to *P. falciparum;* it is less effective against *P. vivax* infections. It is effective against asexual, erythrocytic forms of *P. falciparum,* but not gametocytes of the sexual stage. It is also indicated for treatment of resistant strains of falciparum malaria.
Dose & Administration: For prophylaxis: One 100 mg tablet daily beginning 1-2 days prior to departure to endemic areas, daily during stay in the area, and continued for 4 weeks after departure.

For treatment: Doxycycline (100 mg twice daily for 7 days) or tetracyline (250 mg four times daily for 7 days) given as part of a multi-drug regimen is effective in areas with drug resistant strains of falciparum malaria. Most often used with mefloquine.
Side Effects: Most frequently observed side effects include nausea and epigastric distress; less frequent are incidents of diarrhea and vomiting. Stomach and esophageal ulceration has been reported. The frequency and severity of gastrointestinal side effects may be reduced by taking doxycycline with meals. Absorption of this drug is impaired by antacids containing aluminum, calcium, magnesium, iron, or bismuth subsalicylate. Monilial vaginitis and increased sensitivity to sun exposure are also common side effects.

Halofantrine (Halfan7)

Status: FDA approved for treatment only.
Availability: Currently available in the UK, not yet marketed in the U.S.
Product: A phenanthrenemethanol discovered and developed by Walter Reed Army Institute of Research, and subsequently co-developed by SmithKline Beecham.

Description: 250 mg tablets, indicated for the treatment of mild to moderate malaria caused by *P. falciparum* and *P. vivax* in adults who can tolerate oral medication.

Effectiveness: Halofantrine is effective against chloroquine-sensitive and chloroquine-resistant *P. falciparum*. It is also effective against *P. vivax* and some multi-resistant strains of *P. falciparum*. There may be cross-resistance to mefloquine in certain endemic areas.

Dose & Administration for Treatment: 500 mg (250 mg tablets x 2) every 6 hours for three doses (total first course dose 1500 mg). Repeat this course of therapy in 7 days. Halofantrine should be taken on an empty stomach (no food 2 hours before or 2 hours after each dose).

Side Effects: Generally well tolerated. May cause gastro-intestinal symptoms, including diarrhea. In doses higher than normal or when taken with food containing fat, can cause prolongation of QT interval. Prior treatment with mefloquine increases the likelihood of QT interval prolongation. Can lead to torsade-de-pointes in individuals with congenital prolonged QT syndrome.

Mefloquine HCl (Lariam[R])

Status: FDA approved.

Availability: Currently available.

Product: An anti-malarial drug effective against *P. falciparum* and *P. vivax* infections.

Description: Available as 250 mg tablets.

Effectiveness: Mefloquine HCl provides improved prophylaxis against chloroquine-resistant strains of *P. falciparum* and *P. vivax*. However, *P. falciparum* strains resistant to mefloquine have been reported.

Dose & Administration: For prophylaxis: One 250 mg tablet weekly, beginning 2 weeks prior to departure to endemic areas, and continued for 4 additional weeks after departure.

For treatment: Five 250 mg tablets (15-25 mg/kg) given as a single oral dose. The drug should be taken with at least 8 ounces of water with meals or a snack.

Side Effects: The most frequently observed side effect is vomiting, (3% incidence). It has also been associated with the occurrence of neurologic and psychiatric events after both prophylactic and therapeutic use. Minor neurologic events include dizziness, vertigo, headache, decrease in sleep, visual, and auditory disturbances. Serious adverse events such as seizures, disorientation, and toxic encephalopathy have been reported after therapeutic doses in patients with predisposing medical history (epilepsy, alcohol and drug abuse, or psychiatric disorder). Neurologic side effects have an incidence of less than 1%.

Primaquine Phosphate

Status: FDA approved.
Availability: Currently available.
Product: An anti-malarial drug for elimination of persistent *P. vivax* and *P. ovale* liver stage parasites (hypnozoites).
Description: Available as 26.3 mg (15 mg base) tablets for oral administration.
Effectiveness: Primaquine phosphate is indicated for cure and prevention of relapse of *P. vivax* and *P. ovale* malaria.
Dose & Administration: For treatment and terminal prophylaxis: One tablet daily for 14 days in individuals who are not G-6-PD deficient. The primaquine regimen must overlap at least one dose of chloroquine. Therefore, primaquine must be started no later than 1 week after the last dose of chloroquine.

Current Navy guidance directs that G-6-PD deficient service members are not to be given primaquine. Therefore, if, in the future, use of primaquine in G-6-PD deficient service members is authorized; give three tablets as a single dose once a week for 8 weeks in G-6-PD^{A-} deficient individuals, or two tablets as a single dose once a week for 30 weeks in G-6-PD^{Med} deficient individuals.
Side Effects: The most frequently observed side effects include abdominal discomfort, nausea, headache, interference with visual accommodation, and pruritus. Methemoglobinemia is common, but rarely necessitates interruption of therapy. Leukopenia and agranulocytosis occur rarely. Do not use during pregnancy. If used for treatment in G-6-PD individuals, caution service members of possible side effects (see Chapter 6). If side effects occur, advise members to seek medical evaluation and treatment.

Quinidine Gluconate

Status: FDA approved for treatment of cardiac arrhythmias and intravenous treatment of severe malaria.
Availability: Currently available.

Manufacturer: Generic.

Product: Quinidine is a cinchona alkaloid, the dextrostereoisomer of quinine. Used to treat cardiac arrhythmia, it is now the drug of choice for intravenous treatment of chloroquine-resistant falciparum malaria as intravenous quinine is no longer available in the U.S.

Description: 80 mg/ml (55mg base /ml) intravenous solution available in 10 ml vials as quinidine gluconate.

Effectiveness: Very effective and safe for intravenous treatment of severe malaria. No reports of resistance in any strains of *Plasmodia*.

Dose & Administration: For prophylaxis: Not indicated.

For treatment: Loading dose of 10 mg/kg (6.2 mg base/kg) given over 1-2 hours, followed by continuous infusion of 1.2 mg/kg/hour (0.72 mg base/kg/hour) for 72 hours or until patient can swallow. Intravenous quinidine can safely be administered by monitoring EKG, blood pressure, and infusion speed; quinidine blood levels should be kept between 3-7 mg/L if monitored. Life-threatening arrhythmias are rare with proper doses, but infusion should be stopped temporarily if the EKG shows prolongation of the QRS interval by >50%, or if the QT interval is prolonged >50% of the preceding R-R interval. Hypotension may occur if infusion is too rapid. Loading dose is not indicated if patient started quinine, quinidine, or mefloquine treatment within the preceding 24 hours.

Side Effects: Quinidine is toxic to the heart if given too quickly or in too high a dose. EKG changes including prolonged QT intervals are common, but life threatening arrhythmias are rare if proper dosages are used. Most side effects are gastrointestinal in nature and include nausea, vomiting, abdominal pain, diarrhea, and rarely, esophagitis. Symptoms of mild to moderate cinchonism (ringing in the ears, headache, nausea, and impaired vision) may appear in sensitive patients after one dose of the drug. Less frequent side effects include urticaria, skin flushing with intense itching, and hypersensitivity reactions of angioedema, acute asthmatic episode, and liver toxicity.

Quinine (Quinamm[R])

Status: FDA approved.

Availability: Currently available in the U.S. in tablet form only.

Product: The first successful compound for treatment of malaria, it has been available for three centuries. With the introduction of chloroquine, the use of quinine fell dramatically, but the widespread emergence of chloroquine-resistant *P. falciparum* has increased its use. The intravenous form was last available in the U.S. in 1991.

Description: Available as 130, 200, 260, 300, and 325 mg capsules, and 260 and 325 mg tablets that have a very bitter taste. Indicated for treatment of all forms of malaria in patients able to swallow tablets.

Effectiveness: Acts rapidly against asexual erythrocytic stages of all four *Plasmodium* species that infect humans. There is resistance reported in the rural, northern mountainous area of Thailand and West Africa. Quinine should be used as part of a multi-drug regimen in those areas.

Dose & Administration: For prophylaxis: Not indicated.
For treatment: Adults: 600-650 mg 3 times a day for 7 days.
Children: 10 mg/kg 3 times a day for 7 days.

Side Effects: Quinine has the poorest therapeutic-to-toxic ratio of all of the anti-malarial drugs. Side effects are collectively known as cinchonism and include ringing in the ears, decreased hearing, headache, nausea, vomiting, and mild visual disturbances. These side effects are all dose related and reversible. Less common side effects include urticaria, angioedema of the face, itching, agranulocytosis, hepatitis, and hypoglycemia in patients with high *P. falciparum* parasitemia.

Section 2. Antimalarial Drugs Available in the United States but not in the Military Supply System

Atovaquone

Status: Atovaquone is available as Mepron[R] in the U.S., and is FDA approved for treatment of *Pneumocystis carinii* pneumonia. It is now FDA approved for treatment of malaria.

Availability: Atovaquone was recently introduced in the combination drug Malarone[R] (atovaquone and proguanil) for treatment of malaria. Malarone[R] has been distributed in partnership with WHO under close supervision only to patients resistant to conventional malaria treatment. Malarone[R] is now available in the U.S. for prophylaxis and treatment.

Product: An antiprotozoal agent that is a synthetic derivative of hydroxynaphthoquinone, and may exert its effect by selectively inhibiting electron transport in mitochondria.

Description: Mepron^R (250 mg; intravenous solution,750 mg/5ml), Malarone^R (atovaquone and proguanil).

Effectiveness: Atovaquone is indicated in the acute treatment of mild to moderately severe *Pneumocystis carinii* pneumonia in patients who cannot tolerate co-trimoxazole. Recent trials have shown that a 3 day course of 1000 mg of atovaquone and 400 mg of proguanil had a cure rate of 87% for chloroquine-resistant falciparum malaria.

Dose & Administration: For prophylaxis: One tablet Malarone^R (250 mg atovaquone and 100 mg proguanil) daily. For treatment: For malaria, 1000 mg per day for 3 days in daily combination with 400 mg of proguanil. Atovaquone should be administered with food.

Side Effects. Atovaquone is well tolerated. Common side effects listed in order of occurrence are rash, nausea, diarrhea, headache, fever, and vomiting.

Hydroxychloroquine Sulfate (Plaquenil^R)

Status: FDA approved for prophylaxis and treatment.

Availability: Currently available.

Product: Also a 4-aminoquinoline compound, hydroxychloroquine sulfate has the same actions, effectiveness, and indications as chloroquine phosphate.

Description: 200 mg (155 mg base) tablets.

Effectiveness: L ke chloroquine, it is a blood schizonticide active against *P. vivax, P. malariae, P. ovale*, but with limited activity against most *P. falciparum* infections. It does not prevent relapse in patients with *P. vivax* and *P. ovale* infections, and must be followed with primaquine to effect radical cure of these diseases. As with chloroquine, because of increased parasite resistance, hydroxychloroquine sulfate is considered most useful for prophylaxis in Mexico, Central America, and limited areas of the Middle East.

Dose & Administration: For prophylaxis: Adults: 2 tablets (400 mg) each week beginning 2 weeks prior to exposure, and continued for 4 weeks after leaving endemic area. If unable to begin two weeks prior, an initial double (loading) dose of 4 tablets (800 mg) may be taken in 2 doses 6 hours apart. Children: Administration same as adults; dosage is 5 mg base/kg each week, not to exceed the adult dosage regardless of weight. If unable to begin prophylaxis 2 weeks before exposure, give an initial double (loading) dose of 10 mg base/kg in two doses 6 hours apart.

For treatment: Adults: Initial dose of 4 tablets (800 mg) followed by 2 tablets (400 mg) in 6-8 hours, then 2 tablets (400 mg) on the next 2 days for a total dose of 10 tablets (2000 mg). Children: Four doses as follows; dose 1: 10 mg base/kg; dose 2: 5 mg base/kg 6 hours after dose 1; dose 3: 5 mg base/kg 18 hours after dose 2; dose 4: 5 mg base/kg 24 hours after dose 3.

Side Effects: Usually well tolerated. Side effects reported include mild and transient headache, dizziness, and gastrointestinal complaints of diarrhea, loss of appetite, nausea, abdominal cramps, and rarely, vomiting.

Pyrimethamine/Sulfadoxine (Fansidar^R)

Status: FDA approved for treatment only.

Availability: Currently available.

Product: A combination drug containing the DNA synthesis inhibitors pyrimethamine and sulfadoxine. Each blocks a different enzyme in the synthesis of DNA from guanosine triphosphate.

Description: A tablet containing 25 mg pyrimethamine and 500 mg sulfadoxine.

Effectiveness: Fansidar^R is useful as an alternative treatment of chloroquine-resistant falciparum malaria. It is also often used to treat suspected malaria cases in areas where persons developing malaria symptoms cannot obtain prompt medical evaluation. It once was used as a weekly prophylaxis, but caused frequent, severe allergic reactions. In 1984, American travelers who took Fansidar^R in Kenya were as likely to die from Fansidar^R toxicity as from malaria.

Dose & Administration: For prophylaxis: Not indicated. For treatment: Adults: 3 tablets in a single dose. Children: ¼ tab in those < 1 year old, ½ tab in children 1-3 years old, 1 tab in children 4-8 years old, 2 tabs in adolescents 9-14 years old, 3 tabs in those >14 years old. All treatments, adult and children, are single dose.

Side Effects: Fatalities have occurred due to severe reactions, including Stevens-Johnson syndrome and toxic epidermal necrosis in persons using Fansidar^R as a prophylaxis. No fatal reactions have been reported when it has been used for treatment (3 tablets in a single dose). Adverse reactions, rare when Fansidar^R is used for treatment, include urticaria, serum sickness, itching, conjunctival or scleral injection, nausea, vomiting, headache, and drug fever.

Section 3. Antimalarial Drugs under development or Available in Foreign Countries

Artemisinin

Status: Under investigation.

Availability: Currently used in China and the Far East, not available in the U.S.

Product: A sesquiterpene lactone derived from the Chinese wormwood plant *Artemesia annua*, artemisinin has long been used to treat febrile illnesses in China. There it is known as "qinghaosu."

Description: Artemisinin compounds can be administered enterally, intravenously, or intramuscularly. In China, the drug has been used in the following forms:

Artemisinin suppositories represent a major advantage in treating severe malaria in patients unable to tolerate oral medications in situations where injections cannot be given. They have proved effective in cerebral and other severe falciparum infections. Sodium artesunate is a powder that is reconstituted just before intravenous injection. Artesunate is the tablet form, and has been efficacious in treatment of uncomplicated falciparum malaria. Artemether is the form used for intramuscular injection, and is given in an initial loading dose of 200 mg, followed on the subsequent 6 days with a dose of 100 mg.

Effectiveness: Artemisinin compounds are blood schizonticides effective against parasites resistant to chloroquine and quinine. In a trial in Thailand, artensuate tablets (100 mg initial dose, followed by 50 mg q 12 hrs for 5 days) combined with mefloquine (750 mg initial dose followed by 500 mg after 6 hrs), proved effective in curing adults with uncomplicated falciparum malaria and were more effective than artensuate or mefloquine given alone.

Dose & Administration: For prophylaxis: Not indicated. For treatment: Expected to be effective against all forms of human malaria, particularly severe and complicated falciparum malaria where rapid effects on parasites are needed. Dosage of each is under investigation.

Side Effects: No severe adverse effects have been reported in clinical trials by over 4,000 patients. Mild adverse effects include transient first-degree heart block, mild decreases in reticulocyte and neutrophil counts, elevated liver transaminases, abdominal pain, diarrhea, and drug fever.

Proguanil (Paludrine)

Status: Not approved by the FDA for use.

Availability: Available outside the U.S.

Product: Proguanil is an antifolate agent, and was the first agent found to inhibit dihydrofolate reductase (an enzyme important in DNA synthesis) in plasmodia. It was also recently released as part of the combination drug Malarone^R (Atovaquone and Proguanil).

Description: 100 mg tablets.

Effectiveness: It is useful as a prophylactic agent against *P. falciparum* and *P. vivax*. It acts too slowly to be used alone for treatment of acute malaria, but has been used successfully as part of multi-drug regimens for treatment of uncomplicated malaria. See description of atovaquone for further information.

Dose & Administration: For prophylaxis: 200 mg daily, alone or in combination with chloroquine. For treatment: Useful in multi-drug regimens. Malarone^R (atovaquone and proguanil) given for 3 to 7 days has had success in treatment *of P. ovale, P. malariae*, and multi-drug resistant *P. falciparum.*

Side Effects: Very safe at daily dosage levels. Side effects of nausea, vomiting, abdominal pain, and diarrhea have been experienced at higher dosages.

Pyrimethamine/dapsone (Maloprim^R or Deltaprim^R)

Status: Not released in the U.S.

Availability: The combination drugs Maloprim^R and Deltaprim^R are available in the UK. Pyrimethamine and dapsone are available as individual products in the U.S., but not as combined formulations.

Product: A combination drug containing pyrimethamine and dapsone.

Description: 25 mg pyrimethamine and 100 mg dapsone used as malaria prophylaxis.

Effectiveness: Often prescribed in the UK for suppressive treatment of malaria due to *P. vivax, P. malariae, P. ovale,* and *P. falciparum.* Though toxicity is very uncommon, hemolysis and methemoglobinemia limit the use of this drug. Risk of aplastic anemia limits use for prophylaxis when alternatives are available.

Dose & Administration: For prophylaxis: 1 tablet weekly. For treatment: Not indicated.

Side Effects: Hemolytic anemia, aplastic anemia, methemoglobinemia, Heinz body formation, and bone marrow suppression. Contraindicated in persons with G-6-PD deficiency.

Intravenous Quinine

Status: FDA approved.

Availability: Not available in the U.S. CDC stopped supplying intravenous quinine in 1991.

Product: See description in section 1.

Description: Intravenous concentrations vary, check when formulating intravenous solution for treatment.

Effectiveness: Acts rapidly against asexual erythrocytic stages of all four *Plasmodium* species that infect humans.

Dose & Administration: For prophylaxis: Not indicated.

For treatment: Adults: Loading dose of 20 mg salt/kg given over 4 hours, then followed in 8-12 hours by 10 mg salt/kg given over 4 hours every 8-12 hours until patient can swallow and tolerate oral medication. Children: Loading dose of 15 mg salt/kg given over 2 hours, then followed in 8-12 hours by 10 mg salt/kg given over 2 hours every 12 hours until patient can swallow and tolerate oral medication.

Side Effects: Hypoglycemia is the most common severe side effect of quinine during treatment of malaria. When quinine is being given intravenously, blood glucose levels should be monitored. If there is any change in mental status, hypoglycemia should be suspected. See section 1 for description of other side effects.

WR 238605 (Tafenoquine)

Status: Under investigation.

Availability: Clinical trials only.

Product: This is a new 8-aminoquinoline developed by Walter Reed Army Institute of Research now undergoing clinical trials.

Description: Not applicable.

Effectiveness: Similar in structure to primaquine, in initial tests it appears to be 10 times more active than that drug. It is a tissue schizonticide and has shown some blood schizonticide activity.

Dose & Administration: Pending. It is being developed as a less toxic alternative to primaquine to be used for radical cure of *P. vivax* and *P. ovale* malaria. It is under consideration for potential use for malaria prophylaxis.

Side Effects: There are currently no data on the relative toxicity of this drug compared to primaquine in G-6-PD deficiency.

APPENDIX FIVE

SUPPLIES AND TRAINING AIDS

Following is an extensive list of useful items available through the Federal Supply System for personal protection, chemoprophylaxis, and treatment of malaria. Special circumstances (i.e., new drug development, new patterns of drug resistant plasmodia, significant product improvement, items required due to unique deployment or geographical contingencies) may necessitate purchase of civilian products. The nearest Navy Environmental and Preventive Medicine Unit or Navy Disease Vector Ecology and Control Center are excellent and knowledgeable sources of advice regarding such situations.

Personal Protection Supplies

NSN	ITEM
6840-00-753-4963	Insect repellent, clothing and personal, 75 percent DEET, 2 ounces
6840-01-067-6674	Insecticide, D-phenothrin, 2 percent
6840-01-278-1336	Insect repellent, clothing, Permethrin aerosol, 6 ounce can
6840-01-284-3982	Insect repellent, personal, 33 percent DEET, 2 ounces
7210-01-010-2052	Insect Bar (netting), cot type
7210-00-267-5641	Poles, insect bar (for suspending insect bar)
8415-01-035-0846	Parka, fabric mesh, insect repellent (DEET jacket) – size small
8514-01-035-0847	Parka, fabric mesh, insect repellent (DEET jacket) – size medium

8514-01-035-0848	Parka, fabric mesh, insect repellent (DEET jacket) – size large
8415-00-935-3130	Head net, insect

Antimalarial Drugs

6505-00-117-6450	Chloroquine phosphate tablets, 0.5 gm, 500's
6505-00-913-7905	Chloroquine/Primaquine phosphate tablets, individually sealed, 150's
6505-00-299-8273	Primaquine phosphate tablets, 1000's
6505-01-132-0257	Pyrimethamine-sulfadoxine (Fansidar[R]) tablets, 25's
6505-00-957-9532	Quinine sulfate, 325 mg capsules, 100's
6505-01-095-4175	Doxycycline, 100 mg tablets, 50's
6505-01-078-3717	Chloroquine hydrochloride, injection
6505-00-864-6298	Quinidine gluconate, injection
6505-01-107-1480	Mefloquine hydrochloride, tablets 100's (after stock depleted refer to next stock number)
6505-01-315-1275	Mefloquine hydrochloride, tablets, 25's (use this stock number after previous stock number is depleted)

Training Aids

1. **Bench Aids for the Diagnosis of Malaria.** A set of eight glossy plates, available from World Health Organization Publications Center USA, 49 Sheridan Avenue, Albany, NY 12210. (518) 436-9686. Cost is less than $15.00, which includes shipping and handling.

2. **Audiovisual Aids**

   a) 801472 DN – Vector-Borne Diseases: Our Constant Enemy.

b)   802373 DN – Malaria Prevention

c)   504463 DD – Disease Vector Surveillance and Control in Arid Regions (Still in Development)

d)   802372 DN – Insect Repellent: Do It Yourself Protection From Vector-Borne Disease. (Still in Development)

APPENDIX SIX

GLOSSARY

anemia - decrease in number of red blood cells and/or quantity of hemoglobin. Malaria causes anemia through rupture of red blood cells during merozoite release.

anorexia – lack of appetite, lack of desire or interest in food.

arthralgia – pain or aching of the joints.

chemoprophylaxis – method of disease prevention by taking specific medications. Malaria chemoprophylaxis requires drugs to be taken before, during, and after exposure. Very effective, but not absolute because of drug resistance and poor compliance. Chemoprophylaxis is also called "suppressive treatment."

cinchonism – side effects from quinine or quinidine, reversible with lower dosages or termination of the drugs. Effects include tinnitus, headache, nausea, diarrhea, altered auditory acuity, and blurred vision. The term derives from cinchona bark, the natural source of quinine.

clinical cure – elimination of malaria symptoms, sometimes without eliminating all parasites. See "radical cure" and "suppressive cure."

coma – decreased state of consciousness from which a person cannot be aroused. See "Glasglow coma scale," Table 4-5 in Chapter 4, page 46.

cure – see "clinical cure," "radical cure," and "suppressive cure."

cyanosis, cyanotic – physical sign where the skin appears blue, caused by lack of oxygen.

delirious – mental state characterized by confusion and agitation. Delusions and hallucinations may also be present.

D.O.T. (directly observed therapy) – most effective method of ensuring drug compliance, where drug administration is observed by an appointed authority.

dyspnea – shallow, labored breathing.

eosinophilia – an increased number of eosinophils, a type of white blood cell. Greater than normal numbers of eosinophils are often associated with parasitic infections, but not malaria.

erythrocyte – a red blood cell.

erythrocytic stage – the malaria parasite's life cycle when infecting and developing within red blood cells.

exoerythrocytic stage – stage in plasmodia life cycle when developing in liver cells (hepatocytes).

fever paroxysm – see "paroxysm."

fluid overload – a condition in which an excessive amount of IV fluids (crystalloids, blood products) has been administered. In severe episodes causes pulmonary edema.

fluid resuscitation – administration of IV fluids to correct a loss or decrease in blood volume. The loss may be actual, relative, or both. Actual loss of blood volume is due to hemorrhage, sweating, or diarrhea. Relative loss of blood volume occurs when the vascular system dilates, increasing total volume. Fluid resuscitation is done with a variety of IV fluids, such as normal saline, lactated ringers, dextrose solutions, and blood products.

flush – capillary dilation causing skin to appear reddish in color.

gametocyte – sexual stage of malaria parasites which form in red blood cells. Macrogametocytes (female) and microgametocytes (male) form in individual erythrocytes, are ingested by female mosquitoes, and unite in the mosquito's stomach. Characteristic diagnostic features of *P. falciparum* gametocytes include their crescent or banana shape, and their overshadowing of the morphology of infected red blood cells.

hematemesis – vomiting of blood which may be either acute and bright red; or old and clotted appearing as coffee grounds.

hematochezia – passing blood rectally; blood may appear bright red, or dark red-black, and is usually foul smelling and sticky.

hematocrit – the amount of blood consisting of red blood cells, measured as a percentage. Measured after a blood sample has been centrifuged or allowed to settle. Normal hematocrit values: Males 39-49%; females 33-43%.

hemoglobin – the protein in red blood cells which carries oxygen. Normal range of hemoglobin values: Males – 13.6 - 17.2 g/dl; Females – 12.0 – 15.0 g/dl (136-173 g/L and 120-150 g/L).

hemolysis – destruction of red blood cells. Malaria causes hemolysis when malaria parasites mature and rupture red blood cells they infected.

hepatocytes – liver cells.

hepatomegaly – enlarged liver. An unusual physical finding in malaria.

hyperpyrexia – high fever greater than 105º F (40.5º C).

hyperthermic - elevated temperature.

hypnozoite – a stage of malaria parasites found in liver cells. After sporozoites invade liver cells, some develop into latent forms called hypnozoites. They become active months or years later, producing a recurrent malaria attack. Only *P. vivax* and *P. ovale* species that infect humans develop latent stage hypnozoites. Primaquine is the only available drug active against hypnozoites.

hypoglycemia – blood glucose less than the lower value of normal (70-110 mg/dl [3.9-6.1 mmol/L in SI reference units]). Glucose levels of 40 and below constitute severe hypoglycemia, a life-threatening emergency. Hypoglycemia is common in malaria, as malaria parasitized red blood cells utilize glucose 75 times faster than uninfected cells. In addition, treatment with quinine and quinidine stimulate insulin secretion, reducing blood glucose.

hyponatremia – serum sodium less than the normal lower limit, which is 135-147 mEq/L (135-147 mmol/L in SI reference units). Serum sodium levels approaching 120 and below constitute severe hyponatremia, a medical emergency. Hyponatremia can be seen in malaria, and is indicative of complicated malaria.

hypotension – see "orthostatic hypotension."

icterus – yellow discoloration of the eyes due to an elevated bilirubin. Faint discoloration is seen when bilirubin blood levels rise to 2.5-3.0 mg/dl (43-51 mmol/L in SI reference units). Often identified as scleral icterus, because the sclera or "whites" of the eyes turn yellow.

immunity – the body's ability to control or lessen a malaria attack with antibodies and other protective reactions developed in response to previous malaria attacks. Semi-immune individuals live in malaria endemic areas and are repeatedly infected. Immunity developed does not prevent or cure malaria attacks, but controls the attack, minimizing symptoms. Such individuals typically have low blood levels of malaria parasites.

incubation period – time period beginning when malaria parasites are injected by a mosquito bite, ending when symptoms develop. Incubation periods range from 7 to 40 days, depending on species.

jaundice – yellow discoloration of skin and eyes due to elevated blood levels of bilirubin.

leukocytosis – total white blood cell count greater than 11,000 per cubic millimeter. Leukocytosis refers specifically to elevation in the number of polymorphonuclear leukocytes, which make up the majority of white blood cells.

leukopenia – total white blood cell count of less than 5,000 per cubic millimeter. Leukopenia refers specifically to a reduction in the number of polymorphonuclear leukocytes, which make up the majority of white blood cells.

lymphadenopathy – enlarged lymph nodes, which can be detected by physical examination. Lymphadenopathy is not a usual physical finding in malaria.

malaise – subjective feeling of being sick, ill, or not healthy. The feeling is generalized, varying from mild to severe in intensity. It may be the lone clinical manifestation of malaria, or may accompany other signs and symptoms.

merozoite – the end product of the asexual reproductive stage (schizogony) of the malaria parasite life cycle. Merozoite maturation takes place in erythrocytes or hepatocytes. Schizogony in erythrocytes ends in their rupture, releasing merozoites which infect other red blood cells. Schizogony in liver cells culminates in their rupture and merozoite release, which infect red blood cells. In *P. vivax* and *P. ovale* infections, released merozoites can also infect other liver cells and develop into hypnozoites.

myalgia – muscle pain or ache.

obtunded – mental state in which reaction to stimuli is dulled or blunted, such as persons with severe alcohol intoxication.

oliguria – decrease of urine production.

oocyst – cysts located in the outer stomach wall of mosquitoes, where sporozoite development takes place. When mature, the oocysts rupture and release sporozoites. Sporozoites subsequently migrate to salivary glands, and get injected into the host when mosquitoes feed.

orthostatic hypotension – decrease in blood pressure occurring when an individual arises from a seated or lying position. A small decrease in blood pressure is normal, but large decreases are abnormal, especially if accompanied by clinical manifestations such as faintness, light-headedness, dizziness, or increased pulse. Orthostatic hypotension is a common finding in patients with malaria infections.

parasitemia – level of malaria parasites in blood. If no fever or other symptoms except for an enlarged spleen accompany finding of malaria parasites in blood, the condition is referred to as "asymptomatic parasitemia."

paroxysm – a sudden attack or increase in intensity of a symptom, usually occurring in intervals. Malaria is classically described as producing fever paroxysms; sudden severe temperature elevations accompanied by profuse sweating. However, fever paroxysms are rarely exhibited in the majority of malaria cases in non-immune persons, while semi-immune local inhabitants are more likely to have them. Therefore, diagnosis should not be based on this finding in U.S. military personnel.

petechiae – small red or purple skin macules, usually 1-3 mm in diameter. They are manifestations of small subcutaneous bleeds and seen in minor trauma, when the platelet count is very low, or in clotting defects. They are also caused by immune complex deposits in the skin.

petechial rash – grouping of petechiae.

presumptive treatment – administration of anti-malarial drugs in suspected cases before results of laboratory tests are available to confirm diagnosis.

prophylaxis – see "chemoprophylaxis."

prostration – a state characterized by an extreme loss of strength.

pulmonary edema – accumulation of fluid in lung alveoli due to leakage, resulting in difficulty breathing. It is generally due to breakdown of stability of membranes lining alveolar spaces and/or fluid overload.

QT interval - measured from the beginning of the QRS to the end of the T wave, it represents total duration of ventricular systole. As a rule of thumb, it should be less than 50% of the preceding R-R interval. A prolonged QT interval indicates delayed repolarization of ventricular myocardium. Development of serious ventricular tachyarrhythmias (R on T phenomenon), syncope, and sudden death are possible under this condition.

radical treatment – treatment intended to achieve cure of *P. vivax* or *P. ovale* malaria. Requires primaquine treatment, which destroys latent exoerythrocytic stage parasites (hypnozoites).

radical cure – complete elimination of malaria parasites from the body, specifically hypnozoites.

rales – crackling sounds heard at end inspiration during lung auscultation. An abnormal physical finding.

RBC – red blood cell.

recrudescence – a repeated attack of malaria (short term relapse or delayed), due to the survival of malaria parasites in red blood cells. Characteristic of *P. malariae* infections.

recurrence – a repeated attack weeks, months, or sometimes years, after initial malaria infection, also called a long-term relapse. Due to re-infection of red blood cells from malaria parasites (hypnozoites) that persisted in liver cells (hepatocytes).

relapse – a repeat attack of malaria.

resuscitation – see "fluid resuscitation."

rigor – severe chill, characterized by shaking of the body.

sallow – pale, reddish-yellow in color.

schizogony – asexual reproductive stage of malaria parasites. In red blood cells, schizogony entails development of a single trophozoite into numerous merozoites. A similar process happens in infected liver cells.

scleral icterus – see "icterus."

splenomegaly – an enlarged spleen. A common finding in malaria patients that sometimes can be detected by physical examination.

sporozoite – stage of malaria parasites injected into the bloodstream by biting infective mosquitoes. Sporozoites infect liver cells, disappearing from bloodstream within 30 minutes.

stuporous – mental state characterized by lack of awareness of one's surroundings.

suppressive treatment – treatment intended to prevent clinical symptoms or parasitemia through destruction of parasites in red blood cells. It does not prevent or eliminate malaria infection as parasites may persist in the liver and produce a relapse after drug therapy is stopped. Suppressive treatment is also called "chemoprophylaxis."

tachycardia – increased heart rate, defined as greater than 100 beats per minute.

tachypnea - increased respiratory rate defined as greater than 20 breaths per minute.

thrombocytopenia – low platelet count, defined as less than 150,000. Low platelet counts can lead to impaired blood clotting, and counts below 50,000 increase the risk of spontaneous bleeding.

Thrombocytopenia is typical in malaria, though spontaneous bleeding is rare.

tinnitus – ringing sound in the ears, a common side effect of quinine treatment.

treatment – see "presumptive treatment," "radical treatment," and "suppressive treatment."

trophozoite – early developmental stage of blood schizont.

urticaria – hives. Numerous swellings in skin, ranging from many localized lesions a few mm to a few cm in diameter, to large blotchy irregular swellings.

vasodilation – increase in diameter of small vessels of the vascular system. Net result is often a decrease in blood pressure, which may be significant.

BIBLIOGRAPHY

INTRODUCTION

Bellamy RF, Llewellyn CH. Preventable Casualties: Rommel's Flaw, Slim's Edge. Army 1990 May:52-56.

Smoak BL, DeFraites RF, Magill AJ, Kain KC, Wellde BT. *Plasmodium vivax* infections in U.S. Army troops: Failure of Primaquine to Prevent Relapse in Studies from Somalia. Am J Trop Med Hyg 1997; 56(2):231-234.

World Health Organization, Division of Control of Tropical Diseases. Disease Sheet: Malaria (The Current Situation). World Health Organization web page: www.who.org/programmes/inf/ pub-inf.htm

Stoute JA, Slaoui M, Heppner DG, Momin P, Kester KE, Desmons P, et al. A Preliminary Evaluation of a Recombinant Circumsporo-zoite Protein Vaccine against *Plasmodium Falciparum* Malaria. NEJM 1997, Jan 9;336(2):86-91.

CHAPTER ONE: Malaria: Disease, Life cycle, Distribution

Strickland GT. Malaria. In: Strickland GT, editor. Hunter's Tropical Medicine, 7th Edition. Philadelphia: Saunders; 1991:586-602.

Gilles HM. The Malaria Parasites. In: Gilles HM, Warrell DA, Bruce-Chwatt's Essential Malariology, 3rd Edition. London: Arnold;1993:13-36.

White NJ, Breman JG. Malaria and Babesiosis. In: Isselbacher KJ, Braunwald E, Wilson JD, Martin JB, Fauci AS, Kasper DL, editors.

Harrison's Principles of Internal Medicine, 12th Edition, New York, St. Louis, San Francisco: McGraw-Hill;1994:887-895.

Krogstad DJ. Plasmodium Species (Malaria). In: Mandell GL, Bennet JE, Dolin R, editors. Mandell, Douglas and Bennett's Principles and Practice of Infectious Diseases, 4th Edition. New York: Churchill Livingstone;1995:2415-2426.

Service MW. The Anopheles Vector. In: Gilles HM, Warrell DA, Bruce-Chwatt's Essential Malariology, 3rd Edition. London: Arnold;1993:96-123.

CHAPTER TWO: Prevention

Drugs for Parasitic Infections. The Medical Letter, Vol. 40 (Issue 1017) January 2, 1998.

Sanford Guide to Antimicrobial Therapy, 1997. 27th ed.

Lobel HO, Kozarsky PE. Update on Prevention of Malaria for Travelers. JAMA, December 3, 1997-Vol278, No. 21: 1767-1771.

Legters LJ, Llewellyn CH. Military Medicine. In: Last JM, Wallace RB, editors. Public Health and Preventive Medicine, 13th edition. Norwalk, Connecticut: Saunders; 1992:1141-1157.

Malaria. In: Chin J. Control of Communicable Diseases Manual, 16th Edition. Washington, DC: American Public Health Association, 2000: 310-323.

Strickland GT. Malaria. In: Strickland GT, editor. Hunter's Tropical Medicine, 7th edition. Philadelphia: Saunders; 1991:586-602.

Centers for Disease Control and Prevention. CDC Prevention Guidelines, Specific Recommendations for Vaccinations and Prophylaxis. Atlanta: The Centers for Disease Control;1997:12-17.

United States Navy. Navy Medical Department Guide to Malaria Prevention and Control, 2nd Edition. Norfolk: Navy Environmental Health Center; 1991:52-81.

Bayer R, Wilkinson D. Directly Observed Therapy for Tuberculosis: History of an Idea. Lancet 1995, June 17;345:1545-1548.

CHAPTER THREE: Diagnosis

Warrell DA. Clinical Features of Malaria. In: Gilles HM, Warrell DA, Bruce-Chwatt's Essential Malariology, 3rd Edition. London: Arnold;1993:37-49.

Krogstad DJ. Plasmodium Species (Malaria). In: Mandell GL, Bennet JE, Dolin R, editors. Mandell, Douglas and Bennett's Principles and Practice of Infectious Diseases, 4th Edition. New York: Churchill Livingstone;1995:2415-2426.

Strickland GT. Malaria. In: Strickland GT, editor. Hunter's Tropical Medicine, 7th edition. Philadelphia: Saunders; 1991:586-602.

United States Navy. Navy Medical Department Guide to Malaria Prevention and Control, 2nd Edition. Norfolk: Navy Environmental Health Center; 1991:8-14.

Genton B, Smith T, Baea K, Narara A, Al-Yaman F, Beck HP, et al. Malaria: How Useful are Clinical Criteria for Improving the Diagnosis in a Highly Endemic Area? Tran R S Trop Med Hyg 1994;88:537-541.

CHAPTER FOUR: Treatment

Hoffman, SL: Diagnosis, Treatment, and Prevention of Malaria. Medical Clinics of North America 76:6, 1992.

Barat LM, Bloland PB: Drug Resistance Among Malaria and Other Parasites. Infectious Disease Clinics of North America 11:4, 1997.

Drugs for Parasitic Infections. The Medical Letter, Vol. 40 (Issue 1017) January 2, 1998.

Sanford Guide to Antimicrobial Therapy, 1997. 27th ed.

Malaria. In: Chin J. Control of Communicable Diseases Manual, 17th Edition. Washington, DC: American Public Health Association, 2000:310-323.

Krogstad DJ. Plasmodium Species (Malaria). In: Mandell GL, Bennett JE, Dolin R, editors. Mandell, Douglas and Bennett's Principles and Practice of Infectious Diseases, 4th Edition. New York: Churchill Livingstone;1995:2415-2426.

United States Navy. Navy Medical Department Guide to Malaria Prevention and Control, 2nd Edition. Norfolk: Navy Environmental Health Center; 1991:15-28.

White NJ, Breman JG. Malaria and Babesiosis. In: Isselbacher KJ, Braunwald E, Wilson JD, Martin JB, Fauci AS, Kasper DL, editors. Harrison's Principles of Internal Medicine, 14th Edition, New York, St. Louis, San Francisco: McGraw-Hill;1998:1180-1188.

Warrell DA. Treatment and Prevention of Malaria. In: Gilles HM, Warrell DA, Bruce-Chwatt's Essential Malariology, 3rd Edition. London: Arnold;1993:164-195.

Strickland GT. Treatment and Control of Malaria. In: Strickland GT, editor. Hunter's Tropical Medicine, 8th edition. Philadelphia: Saunders; 2000:614-642.

CHAPTER FIVE: G-6-PD deficiency

Beutler E. Glucose-6-phosphate Dehydrogenase Deficiency and other Enzyme Deficiencies. In: Beutler E, Lichtman MA, Coller BS, Kipps

TJ, editors. Williams Hematology, 5th Edition. New York, St. Louis, San Francisco: McGraw-Hill;1995:564-576.

Lux SE. Hemolytic Anemias IV. Metabolic Disorders. In: Beck WS, editor. Hematology, 3rd Edition, Cambridge, Massachusetts: The MIT Press;1982:215-226.

United States Navy. Navy Medical Department Guide to Malaria Prevention and Control, 2nd Edition. Norfolk: Navy Environmental Health Center; 1991:91-95.

CHAPTER SIX: **Malaria Control Responsibilities**

United States Navy. Navy Medical Department Guide to Malaria Prevention and Control, 2nd Edition. Norfolk: Navy Environmental Health Center; 1991:96-102.

Sanftleben KA. The Joint Medical Officers' Handbook, draft. Bethesda, Maryland: Uniformed Services University of the Health Sciences; 1996.

APPENDIX ONE: **Information & Intelligence Sources, Consultants**

Williams RP. Medical Information Sources for Medical Planners. The Stubby Pencil 1997;10(4):1-6.

Navy Environmental Health Center home page:

http://www-nehc.med.navy.mil

APPENDIX TWO: *Anopheles* Vectors: Identifcation

Service MW. The *Anopheles* Vector. In: Gilles HM, Warrell DA, Bruce-Chwatt's Essential Malariology, 3rd Edition. London: Arnold;1993:96-123.

APPENDIX THREE: Laboratory Diagnostic Techniques

United States Navy. Navy Medical Department Guide to Malaria Prevention and Control, 2nd Edition. Norfolk: Navy Environmental Health Center; 1991:151-157.

Gilles HM. Diagnostic Methods in Malaria. In: Gilles HM, Warrell DA, Bruce-Chwatt's Essential Malariology, 3rd Edition. London: Arnold;1993:78-95.

Shiff CJ, Premji, Minjas JN. The Rapid Manual *Para*Sight^{R}-F test. A New Diagnostic Tool for *Plasmodium Falciparum* Infection. Trans R Soc Trop Med Hyg 1993;87: 646-648.

Singh N, Singh MP, Sharma VP. The Use of a Dipstick Antigen-Capture Assay for the Diagnosis of *Plasmodium Falciparum* Infection in a Remote Forested Area of Central India. Am J Trop Med Hyg 1997;56(2):188-191.

APPENDIX FOUR: Antimalarial medications

Jernigan JA, Pearson RD. Antiparasitic Agents. In: Mandell GL, Bennett JE, Dolin R, editors. Mandell, Douglas and Bennett's Principles and Practice of Infectious Diseases, 4th Edition. New York: Churchill Livingstone;1995:458-475.

United States Army. Medical Products for Supporting Medical Readiness, Vaccines and Drugs, (Go-Book). Ft. Detrick, Maryland: U.S. Army Medical Research and Materiel Command; 1996.

Medical Economics. Physicians' Desk Reference, 51st Edition,1997. Montvale, New Jersey: Medical Economics Data Production Company; 1997.

Antiprotozoal drugs. In: American Medical Association. Drug Evaluations Annual 1994. Chicago: American Medical Association; 1994:1685-1725.

Schlagenhauf P, Lobel H, Steffen R, Johnson R, Popp K, Tschopp A, Letz R, Crevoisier C. Tolerance of Mefloquine by Swissair Trainee Pilots, Am J Trop Med Hyg 1997;56(2):235-240.

APPENDIX FIVE: Supplies and Training Aids

United States Navy. Navy Medical Department Guide to Malaria Prevention and Control, 2nd Edition. Norfolk: Navy Environmental Health Center; 1991:175.

APPENDIX SIX: Glossary

United States Navy. Navy Medical Department Guide to Malaria Prevention and Control, 2nd Edition. Norfolk: Navy Environmental Health Center; 1991:177-182.

DOD INSECT REPELLENT SYSTEM

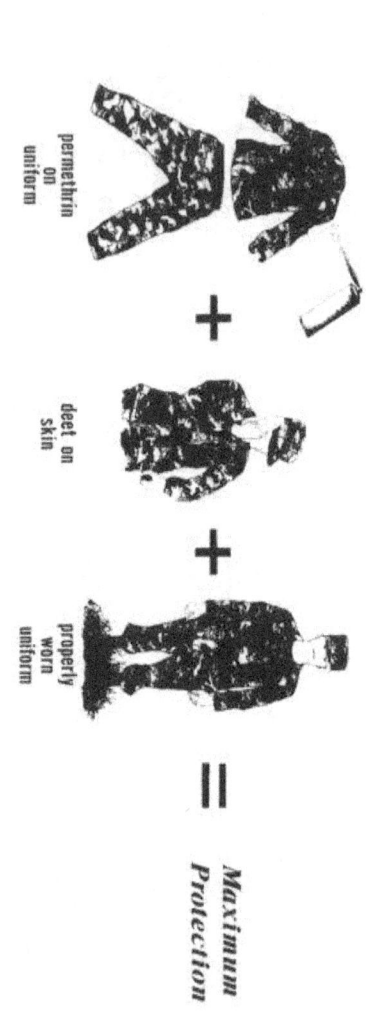

permethrin on uniform

+

deet on skin

+

properly worn uniform

=

Maximum Protection